THE
CASE
FOR
CHRIST

PARTICIPANT'S GUIDE

Resources by Lee Strobel

The Case for Christ
The Case for Christ audio
The Case for Christ — Student Edition (with Jane Vogel)
The Case for Christ curriculum (with Garry Poole)
The Case for Christmas
The Case for Christmas audio
The Case for a Creator
The Case for a Creator audio
The Case for a Creator — Student Edition (with Jane Vogel)
The Case for a Creator curriculum (with Garry Poole)
The Case for Easter
The Case for Faith
The Case for Faith audio
The Case for Faith — Student Edition (with Jane Vogel)
The Case for Faith curriculum (with Garry Poole)
The Case for the Real Jesus
The Case for the Real Jesus audio
Discussing the Da Vinci Code curriculum (with Garry Poole)
Discussing the Da Vinci Code discussion guide (with Garry Poole)
Exploring the Da Vinci Code (with Garry Poole)
Experiencing the Passion of Jesus (with Garry Poole)
Faith Under Fire curriculum series
God's Outrageous Claims
Inside the Mind of Unchurched Harry and Mary
Off My Case for Kids
Surviving a Spiritual Mismatch in Marriage (with Leslie Strobel)
Surviving a Spiritual Mismatch in Marriage audio
What Jesus Would Say

Other Resources by Garry Poole

The Complete Book of Questions
Seeker Small Groups
The Three Habits of Highly Contagious Christians

In the Tough Questions series:

Don't All Religions Lead to God?
How Could God Allow Suffering and Evil?
How Does Anyone Know God Exists?
Why Become a Christian?
Tough Questions Leader's Guide (with Judson Poling)

LEE STROBEL
AND GARRY POOLE

THE
CASE
FOR
CHRIST

PARTICIPANT'S GUIDE

*A Six-Session Investigation on
the Evidence for Jesus*

ZONDERVAN®

ZONDERVAN.com/
AUTHORTRACKER
follow your favorite authors

The Case for Christ Participant's Guide
Copyright © 2008 by Lee Strobel and Garry Poole

Requests for information should be addressed to:

Zondervan, *Grand Rapids, Michigan* 49530

ISBN 978-0-310-28282-2

Interior design by Beth Shagene

Printed in the United States of America

11 12 13 14 • 23 22 21 20 19 18 17 16 15 14 13 12 11 10 9 8 7

CONTENTS

Special thanks to
Laura Allen and Jim Poole
for their outstanding writing and editing contributions.
Their creative insights and suggestions
took this guide to the next level.

THE INVESTIGATION
OF A LIFETIME

For much of my life I was a skeptic. In fact, I considered myself an atheist. To me, there was far too much evidence that God was merely a product of wishful thinking, of ancient mythology, of primitive superstition.... It wasn't a phone call from an informant that prompted me to reexamine the case for Christ. It was my wife.... Eventually I wanted to get to the bottom of what was prompting the subtle but significant shifts in my wife's attitudes, so I launched an all-out investigation into the facts surrounding the case for Christianity.... I applied the training I had received at Yale Law School as well as my experience as legal affairs editor of the Chicago Tribune. And I plunged into the case with more vigor than with any story I had ever pursued.

Lee Strobel, *The Case for Christ*

READ THIS!

If possible, read the following content in preparation for your group meeting. Otherwise, read it as follow-up.

The Case for Christ, introduction: Reopening the Investigation of a Lifetime

WATCH THIS!

DVD Introduction and Teaching Segment #1

For every DVD clip, space is provided to take notes on anything that stands out to you.

DISCUSS THIS!

1. To what degree can you relate to the comments people made about Jesus in the DVD segment? What best represents your current position regarding what you believe about Jesus Christ?

"I don't believe we'll ever know if Jesus was really what everyone says he was. I think it's a lot of folklore. I think it's a lot of historical misrepresentation. It's a lot of wishful thinking. But I don't think we know. I don't think we'll ever know. And I don't think there's any way to prove what has been claimed about Jesus for all these years."

Woman on the street

2. What are your biggest questions or objections regarding Jesus Christ and the Christian faith?

Think About This!

"So, then, Christ may be said to be a fiction in the four senses that (1) it is quite possible that there was no historical Jesus; (2) even if there was, he is lost to us, the result being that there is no historical Jesus available to us; (3) the Jesus who "walks with me and talks with me and tells me I am his own" is an imaginative visualization and in the nature of the case can be nothing more than a fiction; and finally, (4) "Christ" as a corporate logo for this and that religious institution is a euphemistic fiction, not unlike Ronald McDonald, Mickey Mouse, or Joe Camel, the purpose of which is to get you to swallow a whole raft of beliefs, attitudes, and behaviors by an act of simple faith, short-circuiting the dangerous process of thinking the issues out to your own conclusions."

Marshall J. Gauvin, *Did Jesus Christ Really Live?*

"If Jesus Christ is only a human being—no matter how splendid a specimen of humanity he may be—he is part of the problem, not its solution."

British theologian Alister McGrath

"Historically, it is quite doubtful whether Christ ever existed at all, and if he did we do not know anything about him."

Atheist Bertrand Russell

3. What level of confidence do you have that Jesus is an actual histori-cal figure? Or, how confident are you that the existence of Jesus Christ is a matter of legend or wishful thinking? Give reasons behind your response.

"Jesus? I would say no doubt he lived as a person but to the extent of what he did, I'm not sure."

    Woman on the street

4. How possible is it for us to know if Jesus was, in fact, divine? Give reasons for your response. What factors would increase our ability to determine the truth about Jesus' identity?

5. To what extent have you investigated the claims of Christianity prior to this discussion? Describe your experience. What's motivating you to examine these claims today?

6. Describe a bias or self-interest that is at stake for you as you investigate the claims of Jesus. To what degree are you able to discard any preconceptions you may have about him and keep an open mind as you pursue your investigation? Like a juror in a trial, to what extent do you think you will be able to draw conclusions based on the weight of the facts and evidence in this case rather than any prior bias or prejudices?

"I have a lot of different thoughts and theories on Jesus, but I don't think coming back from the dead is really possible."
Man on the street

"If you were selected for a jury in a real trial, you would be asked to affirm up front that you haven't formed any preconceptions about the case. You would be required to vow that you would be open-minded and fair, drawing your conclusions based on the weight of the facts and not on your whims or prejudices. You would be urged to thoughtfully consider the credibility of the witnesses, carefully sift the testimony, and rigorously subject the evidence to your common sense and logic."

Lee Strobel

7. While still an atheist, Lee's initial conclusion was this: *If Christianity is true, it has huge implications for one's life.* What do you think he meant by this statement? Do you agree or disagree with his assessment? Why?

Optional Discussion Questions

- Did you have the opportunity to read the introduction to *The Case for Christ*? Lee Strobel makes the observation that examining the evidence and the facts about Jesus is "the investigation of a lifetime." What do you think is the significance of determining Jesus' identity?

- In the video clip, Lee and Leslie Strobel shared aspects of their spiritual stories. Lee had antagonistic attitudes toward both Christians and Christianity, while Leslie was more neutral about the issues and uncertain about what she believed. Which of the two stories do you relate to most and why?

- Generally speaking, are you driven more by your head or by your heart? To what degree are your questions or objections about God a "heart issue" — as they were for Leslie — and to what degree is your spiritual journey a "head issue," which requires facts and documentation, as for Lee? How might that impact your examination of the evidence for Christ?

- What patterns of church attendance did you establish growing up? How and why has that changed over the years? How would you describe your overall experience with church? If you've never attended a church service before, describe your impressions of what that might be like.

- In what ways do Christians repel you from Christianity? In what ways, if any, do they attract you?

- How would you react if the most important person in your life started attending church regularly and eventually became a Christian? How do you suppose your friends and family members would respond if you one day decided to become a Christian?

- Do you know anyone who has made the decision to become a Christian in the time that you've known them? If so, in what ways has he or she become a different person? How has their decision affected your relationship? What are some of the positive and negative changes that you have observed?

WATCH THIS!

DVD Teaching Segment #2

DISCUSS THIS!

8. In examining a biography, how can you discern between mythical legend and authentic reality? What are some routes of inquiry you might employ to figure this out?

---

*"If Jesus is to be believed —
and I realize that may
be a big if for you at this
point — then nothing is more
important than how you
respond to him."*

Lee Strobel

Think About This!

One Solitary Life

He was born in an obscure village, the child of a peasant woman. He grew up in another obscure village, where he worked in a carpenter shop until he was thirty. Then for three years he was an itinerant preacher. He never had a family or owned a home. He never set foot inside a big city. He never traveled two hundred miles from the place he was born. He never wrote a book, or held an office. He did none of the things that usually accompany greatness.

While he was still a young man, the tide of popular opinion turned against him. His friends deserted him. He was turned over to his enemies and went through the mockery of a trial. He was nailed to a cross between two thieves. While he was dying, his executioners gambled for the only piece of property he had—his coat.

When he was dead, he was taken down and laid in a borrowed grave.

Nineteen long centuries have come and gone, and today he is the central figure for much of the human race. All the armies that ever marched, and all the navies that ever sailed, and all the parliaments that ever sat, and all the kings that ever reigned, put together, have not affected the life of man upon this earth as powerfully as that one solitary life.

Author unknown

9. What do you believe about Jesus? Was he a great moral teacher? Was he a prophet? Did he possess special powers? Was he God in human form or was he simply a good man that legend has elevated to the status of the divine?

10. Did Jesus really claim to be God? What did his followers of that era believe about his identity? What have you heard or read about the divinity of Jesus?

11. If Jesus did claim to be God in human form, as the Bible states, can this assertion ever be proven to your satisfaction? Short of Jesus showing up tonight in physical form, could there ever be enough evidence to convince you of his true identity? Why or why not? Is it realistic to say his identity could ever be proven based on a preponderance of the evidence? Elaborate.

✝ Think About This!

"A man who was merely a man and said the sort of things Jesus said would not be a great moral teacher. He would either be a lunatic—on the level with the man who says he is a poached egg—or else he would be the Devil of Hell. You must make your choice. Either this was, and is, the Son of God; or else a madman or something worse. You can shut him up for a fool, you can spit at him and kill him as a demon, or you can fall at his feet and call him Lord and God. But let us not come with any patronizing nonsense about his being a great human teacher. He has not left that open to us. He did not intend to."

C. S. Lewis, *Mere Christianity*

12. Jesus once asked his disciples "Who do the crowds say I am?" and he received a variety of responses (see Luke 9:18–19). At this point in your spiritual investigation, who do *you* say Jesus is? On a scale from 1 to 10 (1 = I'm very certain Jesus was an extraordinary man, but he was not God in human form; 5 = I'm in a fog concerning who Jesus was; 10 = I'm very certain Jesus was God in human form just as he claimed he was), place an X near the spot that best describes you. Then share your selection with the rest of the group and give reasons for placing your X where you did.

1	2	3	4	5	6	7	8	9	10

Jesus—a great man
but not God

Unsure who Jesus was

Jesus—God
in human form

"Jesus made it clear by word and deed that to know him was to know God, to see him was to see God, to believe in him was to believe in God, to receive him was to receive God, to reject him was to reject God, and to honor him was to honor God."

British theologian John Stott

Optional Discussion Questions

- What is your assessment of the Bible? Is it a trustworthy historical document? Does it have any spiritual value? Give reasons for your answers.

- Regardless of whether or not you believe the Bible to be true, many have observed that it is a remarkable and beautiful piece of literature that has influenced countless generations. Aside from its potential spiritual value, is this reason enough to read and study it? Why or why not?

- If it could be demonstrated that the Bible is an extremely well-preserved and factual historical document upon which historians and archaeologists rely, what weight would you then give to the information it contains and the implications for your life?

- To what degree of accuracy do you think historical records reflect actual past occurrences? What factors determine the level of accuracy of historical documents?

- Can we ever really know the historical truth about Jesus? Why or why not? What factors would increase the accuracy of our understanding of who Jesus is?

WATCH THIS!

DVD Wrap-up/Lee's Perspective

BETWEEN SESSIONS

Personal Reflection

It was now winter, and Jesus was in Jerusalem at the time of Hanukkah. He was at the Temple, walking through the section known as Solomon's Colonnade. The Jewish leaders surrounded him and asked, "How long are you going to keep us in suspense? If you are the Messiah, tell us plainly."

Jesus replied, "I have already told you, and you don't believe me. The proof is what I do in the name of my Father. But you don't believe me because you are not part of my flock. My sheep recognize my voice; I know them, and they follow me. I give them eternal life, and they will never perish. No one will snatch them away from me, for my Father has given them to me, and he is more powerful than anyone else. So no one can take them from me. The Father and I are one."

Once again the Jewish leaders picked up stones to kill him. Jesus said, "At my Father's direction I have done many things to help the people. For which one of these good deeds are you killing me?" They replied, "Not for any good work, but for blasphemy, because you, a mere man, have made yourself God."

John 10:22–33 NLT

- Prior to this study session, when was the last time you gave more than a cursory thought to the person known as Jesus Christ? Who is Jesus? What impact has he had in your life? And how did this humble man from the Middle East manage to revolutionize the entire known world in such a dramatic way that his very birthday divides all of history right down the middle?

- What are some other ways Jesus has had influence—either positive or negative? How well have Christians followed the ways of Jesus? The Bible claims to contain his teachings, but have his words and his legacy been properly preserved? Are the first four books of the New Testament—Matthew, Mark, Luke, and John—accurate biographies of the life and teachings of Jesus? How can you be sure either way?

- According to John 10:22–33 above, what did Jesus appear to believe about himself? What do you think his followers believed about him? What did the religious leaders of that time believe about him? It is a matter of historical record that Jesus was later crucified and buried. The Bible records that this punishment was handed down, in part, for the charge of blasphemy—for his claim to be God. Did Jesus really believe he was God? If so, what conclusions can you draw about him? Was he telling the truth? British philosopher C. S. Lewis famously proposed that Jesus was either a legend, liar, lunatic, or the Lord God. Are there any other options? Would a sane, truthful, good person falsely claim to be God? How open are you to discovering the identity of Jesus for yourself once and for all? What is the driving force behind your search? What difference might it make in your life? And how committed are you to be open-minded and fair, drawing your conclusions based on the weight of the facts and evidence presented in this case?

• Perhaps you can take some time right now to further reflect on these verses written by the disciple John. Assuming this account has been preserved accurately, does it have anything new to teach you that you didn't already know about Jesus? Are you willing to say a short prayer right now to invite God to reveal the truth about Jesus to you in the coming days?

EYEWITNESS EVIDENCE

But all I had ever really given the evidence was a cursory look. I had read just enough philosophy and history to find support for my skepticism – a fact here, a scientific theory there, a pithy quote, a clever argument... Setting aside my self-interest and prejudices as best I could, I read books, interviewed experts, asked questions, analyzed history, explored archaeology, studied ancient literature, and for the first time in my life picked apart the Bible verse by verse.

Lee Strobel, *The Case for Christ*

READ THIS!

If possible, read the following content in preparation for your group meeting. Otherwise, read it as follow-up.

The Case for Christ, chapter 1: The Eyewitness Evidence

The Case for Christ, chapter 2: Testing the Eyewitness Evidence

The Case for Christ, chapter 3: The Documentary Evidence

WATCH THIS!

DVD Teaching Segment #1

For every DVD clip, space is provided to take notes on anything that stands out to you.

DISCUSS THIS!

1. What's your assessment of the Bible? Is it mostly accurate, partly accurate, or mostly inaccurate? Give reasons for your response.

"All Bibles are man-made."

Thomas Edison

Think About This!

"If we can have confidence that the Gospels were written by the disciples Matthew and John, by Mark, the companion of the disciple Peter, and by Luke, the historian, companion of Paul, and a first-century journalist, we can be assured that the events they record are based on either direct or indirect eyewitness testimony."

Lee Strobel

"Few intelligent Christians can still hold to the idea that the Bible is an infallible book, that it contains no linguistic errors, no historical discrepancies, no antiquated scientific assumptions, not even bad ethical standards. Historical investigation and literary criticism have taken the magic out of the Bible and have made it a composite human book, written by many hands in different ages. The existence of thousands of variations of texts makes it impossible to hold the doctrine of a book verbally infallible."

Elmer Homrighausen, former dean of Princeton Theological Seminary

2. Do you think it's really possible to be an intelligent, critically thinking person and believe that the four gospels were written within a generation of Jesus by the actual people whose names have been attached to them? Why or why not?

3. Do you agree that the Bible is a set of ancient historical documents to which historians can apply the same criteria for determining whether or not *any* historical record is accurate? Elaborate.

Think About This!

"But what eyewitness accounts do we possess? Do we have the testimony of anyone who personally interacted with Jesus, who listened to his teachings, who saw his miracles, who witnessed his death, and who perhaps even encountered him after his alleged resurrection? Do we have any records from first-century 'journalists' who interviewed eyewitnesses, asked tough questions, and faithfully recorded what they scrupulously determined to be true? Equally important, how well would these accounts withstand the scrutiny of skeptics?"

Lee Strobel

"We have actually very early attestation of the authorship of the Gospels. The early church father Papias, for example, as recorded by the church historian Eusebius, identifies Mark's gospel as essentially the eyewitness account of Peter. Papias was a disciple of the apostle John, so we are only one generation removed from Jesus himself. Now that is a pretty close testimony and strongly suggesting that the Gospels are based on eyewitness accounts."

New Testament scholar Mark Strauss

"It has become evident to scholars of the first century that the Gospels were actually attempts to write biographies of Jesus. They are very clearly attempts by eyewitnesses to describe exactly what Jesus said and did, and the consensus of New Testament scholarship has moved in that direction."

Theologian and apologist J. P. Moreland

4. Do you believe the author Luke intended to record the truth concerning Jesus? What about the other first-century writers of the New Testament? What motives might cause these writers to distort the historical record? Explain your opinion.

Think About This!

"Luke's gospel begins with a prologue; it is actually one of the finest Greek sections in the whole New Testament. Luke was clearly a literary artist, but in that prologue he points out that he has carefully investigated the material that he presents in the Gospels, that he has checked with eyewitness accounts, those who were actually present. If you read that prologue, you see that this is the work of a historian. This was someone who has done his research."

Mark Strauss

5. Read the introduction to the gospel of Luke, below. Would you agree or disagree that this appears to be the work of a biographer who has done his research? Elaborate.

> *Many have undertaken to draw up an account of the things that have been fulfilled among us, just as they were handed down to us by those who from the first were eyewitnesses and servants of the word. With this in mind, since I myself have carefully investigated everything from the beginning, I too decided to write an orderly account for you, most excellent Theophilus, so that you may know the certainty of the things you have been taught.*
>
> Luke 1:1–4

"If God wanted to send us a message, and ancient writings were the only way he could think of doing it, he could have done a better job."
Dr. Arroway in Carl Sagan's film *Contact*

6. Mark Strauss suggests that the four New Testament Gospels or biographies of Jesus (Matthew, Mark, Luke, and John), all written in the first century, are our earliest and most reliable records of Jesus. Since they were written remarkably close to the actual occurrence of the events themselves, eyewitnesses still living and present would have objected to any inaccuracies, making the Gospels unlikely to be corrupted by legend and wishful thinking. Do you agree or disagree with Strauss's logic? Why?

Think About This!

"Consider the way the Gospels are written—in a sober and responsible fashion, with accurate incidental details, with obvious care and exactitude. You don't find the outlandish flourishes and blatant mythologizing that you see in a lot of other ancient writings."

New Testament scholar Craig Blomberg

7. How does the fact that the four Gospels are rooted in eyewitness testimony, and written in a sober fashion with accurate incidental details that can be confirmed by archaeology, influence your assessment of the reliability of their records?

Optional Discussion Questions

- How much of the related chapters in *The Case for Christ* were you able to read? Was there anything from these chapters that influenced your opinion of the authenticity of the biographies of Jesus?

- Short of seeing it with your own eyes, how can you ever really know for sure that an event actually occurred? How are you able to verify everyday occurrences without actually observing them?

- What are the pros and cons of "eyewitness testimony"? How trustworthy do you think it can ever really be? How important is it in determining the facts of any case? What factors might help you weigh whether any particular eyewitness account is accurate?

- Can the testimony of ancient eyewitnesses be trusted to be historically accurate? Why or why not? To what extent do you think it is possible to verify the truth of the Bible at this late date?

WATCH THIS!

DVD Teaching Segment #2

> "If one were to take the Bible
> seriously, one would go mad.
> But to take the Bible seriously,
> one must be already mad."
> British writer Aleister Crowley

DISCUSS THIS!

8. Put yourself into the ancient world—a world without modern media and where the standard way of preserving information was through oral tradition that people memorized. How would you "improve" on the oral tradition in this ancient world scenario? What types of measures would you take to ensure that the story you told remained intact and accurately preserved? How do you think oral history and written history differ? Is one method necessarily more accurate than the other? Explain.

"In our day of instant media ... everything has to be on film or tape recorded. We are more skeptical of oral tradition, but we don't really understand the nature of oral tradition. Oral tradition is a community event. A story is passed down by individuals within that community.... Well, if they get it wrong, you've got an entire community that is going to correct them. So it is self-correcting all the way."

Mark Strauss

9. How is your view of the level of accuracy behind the oral tradition influenced by the fact that in the tradition of the Jews—the culture in which Jesus lived—information was painstakingly and accurately preserved to the point that young rabbis were often forbidden to comment on a passage of Scripture until they had memorized it perfectly? In what ways does this approach differ from the game of "telephone" mentioned in the DVD clip? Elaborate.

"Some scholars say the Gospels were written so far after the events that legend developed and distorted what was finally written down, turning Jesus from merely a wise teacher into the mythological Son of God."
Lee Strobel

Think About This!

"One of the arguments I'd often heard against believing what the Gospels say is that they contradict one another. How can two Gospels both be accurate if they give different accounts of the same event? A surprising discovery is that many historians consider minor variations to be evidence in favor of the truth of an account. The idea is that if the writers were lying, they'd make sure to get their stories straight—and they'd agree in every detail. What seems to be a contradiction is often just the same event viewed from a different perspective."
Lee Strobel

10. To what extent have you heard or do you believe that the Bible is full of contradictions? Describe one or two contradictions you know are found in the Bible. Do you think there are any irreconcilable discrepancies among the four gospel accounts? Why or why not? How does your answer impact your view of the accuracy and reliability of the Bible?

Contradictory Evidence?

The four biographies of Jesus—Matthew, Mark, Luke, and John—don't always tell the same story in exactly the same way. Following are two examples and possible explanations.

Story	Contradiction?	Possible Explanation
Jesus heals a Roman centurion's servant (described in Matthew 8:5–13 and Luke 7:1–10).	• Matthew says that the centurion asked Jesus to heal his servant. • Lukes says that the centurion sent others to ask Jesus to heal the servant.	Just as we might say, "The President announced a new foreign policy today," when actually the announcement was written by a speechwriter and delivered by the press secretary, so in New Testament times people would say that an official (like the centurion) did something, even though he did it through others.
Jesus' genealogies (found in Matthew 1:1–16 and Luke 3:23–38)	Different people are listed in the two genealogies.	Matthew gives Joseph's side of the family tree; Luke gives Mary's side of the family tree.

If you're interested in studying other apparent contradictions in the New Testament for yourself, consider either *The Encyclopedia of Biblical Difficulties* by Gleason L. Archer or *When Critics Ask* by Norman Geisler and Thomas Howe.

"There is enough of a discrepancy to show that there could have been no previous concert among the [Gospel writers]; and at the same time such substantial agreement as to show that they all were independent narrators of the same great transaction."

Simon Greenleaf, Harvard Law School

Think About This!

"When I hold a Bible in my hands, essentially I'm holding copies of ancient historical records. The original manuscripts of the biographies of Jesus — Matthew, Mark, Luke, and John — and all the other books of the Old and New Testaments have long ago crumbled into dust. So how can I be sure that these modern-day versions — the end product of countless copying throughout the ages — bear any resemblance to what the authors originally wrote? When I first found out that there are no surviving originals of the New Testament, I was really skeptical. I thought, if all we have are copies of copies of copies, how can I have any confidence that the New Testament we have today bears any resemblance whatsoever to what was originally written?"

Lee Strobel

11. To what extent do you think the information contained in the original Bible manuscripts has been reliably copied and accurately translated into our current Bible? How much do you trust that the Bible you read today is an accurate reflection of the original writings?

Think About This!

"The more often you have copies that agree with each other, especially if they emerge from different geographical areas, the more you can cross-check them to figure out what the original document was like. The only way they'd agree would be where they went back genealogically in a family tree that represents the descent of the manuscripts. The quantity of New Testament material is almost embarrassing in comparison with other works of antiquity."

Bruce Metzger, professor emeritus, Princeton Theological Seminary

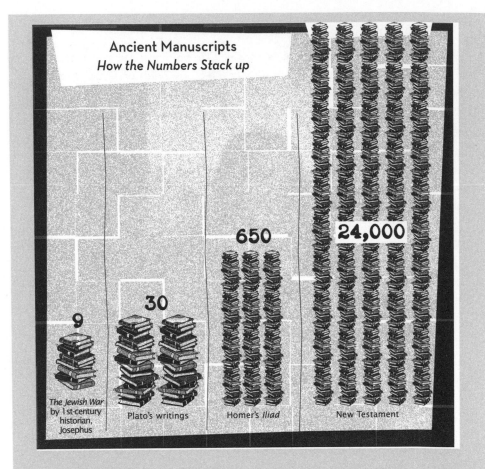

Ancient Manuscripts
How the Numbers Stack up

9
The Jewish War by 1st-century historian, Josephus

30
Plato's writings

650
Homer's *Iliad*

24,000
New Testament

"There is no comparison: the manuscript evidence for the New Testament is overwhelming when juxtaposed against other revered writings of antiquity — works that modern scholars have absolutely no reluctance treating as authentic. The grand total of Greek manuscripts is at 5,664. In addition to the Greek documents there are thousands of other ancient New Testament manuscripts in other languages. There are 8,000 to 10,000 Latin Vulgate manuscripts, plus a total of 8,000 in Ethiopic, Slavic, and Armenian. In all, there are about 24,000 manuscripts in existence."

Lee Strobel

12. How does the fact that there are virtually 24,000 copies of New Testament manuscripts affect your opinion about whether the texts we have are accurate?

Think About This!

"Books—or actually, scrolls of papyrus—were relatively rare. Therefore education, learning, worship, teaching in religious communities—all this was done by word of mouth. Rabbis became famous for having the entire Old Testament committed to memory. So it would have been well within the capability of Jesus' disciples to have committed much more to memory than appears in all four Gospels put together—and to have passed it along accurately."

New Testament scholar Craig Blomberg

"The New Testament, then, has not only survived in more manuscripts than any other book from antiquity, but it has survived in a purer form than any other great book—a form that is 99.5 percent pure."

Norman Geisler and William Nix

"I've made a hobby of collecting alleged discrepancies, inaccuracies, and conflicting statements in the Bible. I have a list of about eight hundred of them. A few years ago I coauthored a book called When Critics Ask, which devotes nearly six hundred pages to setting the record straight. All I can tell you is that in my experience when critics raise these objections, they invariably violate one of seventeen principles for interpreting Scripture."

Norman Geisler, founder, Southern Evangelical Seminary

"It ain't the parts of the Bible that I can't understand that bother me; it is the parts that I do understand."

Mark Twain

Optional Discussion Questions

- Given your understanding of the oral tradition, how likely is it that the information and events recorded in the New Testament have been reliably preserved between the time they occurred and the time they were actually written down?

- Scholar J. P. Moreland points out that we have virtually the entire New Testament preserved in the historical quotations of the church fathers of the first four centuries, so that even if we had no copies of the New Testament, we could reconstruct it from just these quotes. How does this additional fact affect your opinion of the reliability of the New Testament document we do have today?

- When you compare three or four different newspaper accounts of a national story, how similar or dissimilar are the details of the story? How accurate an image of the event do you get? What happens when three or four different witnesses view the same car accident from slightly different angles? To what extent would the details of the report differ with each person's testimony? Explain how and why this happens.

- If the biblical authors were in collusion to create a false testimony, why do you think they didn't plan more carefully and make the incidental details of their accounts more similar? Do you agree with the supposition that if the Gospels were too consistent, that fact would invalidate them as independent witnesses? Why or why not?

"In no other case is the interval of time between the composition of the book and the date of the earliest manuscripts so short as in that of the New Testament."

British classical scholar Sir Frederic Kenyon

WATCH THIS!

DVD Wrap-up/Lee's Perspective

> *"The last foundation for any doubt that the Scriptures have come down to us substantially as they were written has now been removed."*
>
> Sir Frederic Kenyon

BETWEEN SESSIONS

Personal Reflection

In my former book, Theophilus, I wrote about all that Jesus began to do and to teach until the day he was taken up to heaven, after giving instructions through the Holy Spirit to the apostles he had chosen. After his suffering, he presented himself to them and gave many convincing proofs that he was alive. He appeared to them over a period of forty days and spoke about the kingdom of God.

Acts 1:1–3

- Read the above introduction to the book of Acts, written by Luke. In it, he refers to his "former book," which, like Acts, was also written as a letter. Does Luke seem to be sincere in his explanation for writing these letters to Theophilus? What kind of information does Luke report? Does he appear to believe his account himself? What do you suppose might be his level of concern for accuracy? Do you believe he intended to be truthful?

• The second chapter of Luke begins:

> *In those days Caesar Augustus issued a decree that a census should be*
> *taken of the entire Roman world. (This was the first census that took place*
> *while Quirinius was governor of Syria.) And everyone went to their own*
> *town to register. So Joseph also went up from the town of Nazareth in*
> *Galilee to Judea, to Bethlehem the town of David, because he belonged*
> *to the house and line of David.*
>
> Luke 2:1–4

Does Luke include any specific details that might be verifiable two thousand years later? If so, which ones? Why do you suppose he includes this information? Are you surprised to learn that the Bible is full of such verifiable historical details? What do you think it would take for you to believe that the Bible is a reliable historical document that was handed down with accuracy? What implications would result if you learned that corroborative evidence exists to support the detailed information that the Bible contains?

• Consider which questions and doubts about the accuracy of the Bible have been addressed so far. What questions still remain or have arisen for you? Are you interested in further pursuing the answers to your questions and doubts? What additional steps could you take to resolve these issues?

• Be honest with yourself, and consider how your confidence in the Bible has been affected by this session. Are your heart and mind more or less open to the possibilities? What would it take to convince you that the Bible is a trustworthy historical document? And further, what would it take to convince you that the Bible is a trustworthy *spiritual* document? Have you ever considered reading it? Why not start now, beginning with the book of Luke? Would you at this moment say a short prayer and ask God to open your heart and mind to the truth about the Bible?

EVIDENCE OUTSIDE THE BIBLE

What if there were other biographies of Jesus that have been censored because the early church didn't like the image of Jesus they portrayed? How could I have confidence that church politics haven't squelched biographies of Jesus that were every bit as accurate as the four that were finally included in the New Testament, and that would shed important new light on the words and deeds of this controversial carpenter from Nazareth?... If the Jesus of faith is not also the Jesus of history, he's powerless and he's meaningless. Unless he's rooted in reality, unless he established his divinity by rising from the dead, he's just a feel-good symbol who's as irrelevant as Santa Claus.

Lee Strobel, *The Case for Christ*

READ THIS!

If possible, read the following content in preparation for your group meeting. Otherwise, read it as follow-up.

The Case for Christ, chapter 4: The Corroborating Evidence
The Case for Christ, chapter 6: The Rebuttal Evidence

WATCH THIS!

DVD Teaching Segment #1

For every DVD clip, space is provided to take notes on anything that stands out to you.

DISCUSS THIS!

1. Was Jesus a real person in history? Give a brief historical description of the general events surrounding his life and death.

"We also have volumes of writings by the 'apostolic fathers,' who were the earliest Christian writers after the New Testament. They authored the Epistle of Clement of Rome, the Epistles of Ignatius, the Epistle of Polycarp, the Epistle of Barnabas, and others. In many places these writings attest to the basic facts about Jesus, particularly his teachings, his crucifixion, his resurrection, and his divine nature."

Lee Strobel

Fast Fact

Corroborative Evidence

Webster's dictionary defines corroborate this way: "To make more certain; confirm: He corroborated my account of the accident."

Corroborative evidence supports other testimony; it affirms or backs up the essential elements of an eyewitness account. It can be a public record, a photograph, or additional testimony from a second or third person. It can verify a person's entire testimony or just key parts of it. In effect, corroborative evidence acts like the support wires that keep a tall antenna straight and unwavering. The more corroborative evidence, the stronger and more secure the case.

2. Describe an incident in which you doubted someone's story until he or she offered some corroborating evidence. What criteria helped you determine the level of relevancy of this supporting evidence?

"If the New Testament were a collection of secular writings, their authenticity would generally be regarded as beyond all doubt."

Historian F. F. Bruce

Think About This!

"Let's pretend we didn't have any of the New Testament or other Christian writings. Even without them, what would we be able to conclude about Jesus from ancient non-Christian sources, such as Josephus, the Talmud, Tacitus, Pliny the Younger, and others?"

Lee Strobel

"Often the same people, places, and events referenced inside Scripture are cited also in non-biblical materials. These range from a myriad of geographical place names to the hard evidence by archaeology to a host of documents that have come down to us from the ancient world that correlate completely with the biblical evidence."

Historian Paul Maier, Western Michigan University

"We would still have a considerable amount of important historical evidence [about Jesus without the New Testament]; in fact, it would provide a kind of outline for the life of Jesus. We would know that first, Jesus was a Jewish teacher; second, many people believed that he performed healings and exorcisms; third, some people believed he was the Messiah; fourth, he was rejected by the Jewish leaders; fifth, he was crucified under Pontius Pilate in the reign of Tiberius; sixth, despite this shameful death, his followers, who believed that he was still alive, spread beyond Palestine so that there were multitudes of them in Rome by AD 64; and seventh, all kinds of people from the cities and countryside—men and women, slave and free—worshiped him as God."

Historian Edwin M. Yamauchi, Miami (Ohio) University

"This was indeed an impressive amount of independent corroboration. And not only can the contours of Jesus' life be reconstructed apart from the Bible, but there's even more that can be gleaned about him from material so old that it actually predates the Gospels themselves."

Lee Strobel

Think About This!

Josephus

"Josephus was a very important Jewish historian of the first century. He was born in AD 37, and he wrote most of his four works toward the end of the first century. He was a priest, a Pharisee, and he was somewhat egotistical. His most ambitious *work was called The Antiquities, which was a history of the Jewish people from Creation until his time. He probably completed it in about AD 93."*

Edwin M. Yamauchi

"He [Ananias] convened a meeting of the Sanhedrin and brought before them a man named James, the brother of Jesus, who was called the Christ, and certain others. He accused them of having transgressed the law and delivered them up to be stoned."

Josephus, The Antiquities

"Now there was about this time Jesus, a wise man, for he was a doer of wonderful works, a teacher of such men as received the truth with pleasure. He drew over to him both many of the Jews and many of the Gentiles. When Pilate, at the suggestion of the principle men amongst us, had condemned him to the cross, those that loved him first did not forsake him. And the tribe of Christians so named for him are not extinct to this day."

Josephus, Testimonium Flavianum

"Josephus corroborates important information about Jesus: that he was the martyred leader of the church in Jerusalem and that he was a wise teacher who had established a wide and lasting following, despite the fact that he had been crucified under Pilate at the instigation of some of the Jewish leaders. [Josephus'] accounts of the Jewish War have proved to be very accurate; for example, they've been corroborated through archaeological excavations at Masada as well as by historians like Tacitus. He's considered to be a pretty reliable historian, and his mentioning of Jesus is considered extremely important."

Edwin M. Yamauchi

3. How does the fact that the Jewish historian, Josephus, gives accurate accounts of other historical details support his accounts of Jesus and the early Christians?

Think About This!

Tacitus

"Tacitus recorded what is probably the most important reference to Jesus outside the New Testament. In AD 115 he explicitly states that Nero persecuted the Christians as scapegoats to divert suspicion away from himself for the great fire that had devastated Rome in AD 64."

Edwin M. Yamauchi

"Nero fastened the guilt and inflicted the most exquisite tortures on a class hated for their abominations, called Christians by the populace. Christus, from whom the name had its origin, suffered the extreme penalty during the reign of Tiberius at the hands of one of our procurators, Pontius Pilatus, and a most mischievous superstition, thus checked for the moment, again broke out not only in Judaea, the first source of the evil, but even in Rome.... Accordingly, an arrest was first made of all who pleaded guilty: then, upon their information, an immense multitude was convicted, not so much of the crime of firing the city, as of hatred against mankind."

Tacitus, Annals

4. How does the fact that Tacitus does not align himself with Christians affect your confidence in the reliability of his "outside" evidence for Jesus? Do you think he was trying to promote Christianity in any way? Do you think he believed that Jesus was a real historical figure?

"The Bible is a book that has been read more and examined less than any book that ever existed."

The Theological Works of Thomas Paine

Think About This!

Pliny the Younger

"[Pliny the Younger] was the nephew of Pliny the Elder, the famous encyclopedist who died in the eruption of Vesuvius in AD 79. Pliny the Younger became governor of Bithynia in northwestern Turkey. Much of his correspondence with his friend, Emperor Trajan, has been preserved to the present time."

Edwin Yamauchi

"I have asked them if they are Christians, and if they admit it, I repeat the question a second and third time, with a warning of the punishment awaiting them. If they persist, I order them to be led away for execution; for, whatever the nature of their admission, I am convinced that their stubbornness and unshakable obstinacy ought not to go unpunished.... They also declared that the sum total of their guilt or error amounted to no more than this: they had met regularly before dawn on a fixed day to chant verses alternately amongst themselves in honor of Christ as if to a god, and also to bind themselves by oath, not for any criminal purpose, but to abstain from theft, robbery, and adultery.... This made me decide it was all the more necessary to extract the truth by torture from two slave-women, whom they called deaconesses. I found nothing but a degenerate sort of cult carried to extravagant lengths."

Pliny the Younger, Letters

Tertullian and Phlegon

"To me, one of the most problematic references in the New Testament is where the Gospel writers claim that the earth went dark during part of the time that Jesus hung on the cross. Wasn't this merely a literary device to stress the significance of the crucifixion, and not a reference to an actual historical occurrence? After all, if darkness had fallen over the earth, wouldn't there be at least some mention of this extraordinary event outside the Bible?"

Lee Strobel

"This phenomenon, evidently, was visible in Rome, Athens, and other Mediterranean cities. According to Tertullian ... it was a 'cosmic' or 'world event.' Phlegon, a Greek author from Caria writing a chronology soon after 137 AD, reported that in the fourth year of the 202nd Olympiad (i.e., 33 AD) there was 'the greatest eclipse of the sun' and that 'it became night in the sixth hour of the day [i.e., noon] so that stars even appeared in the heavens. There was a great earthquake in Bithynia, and many things were overturned in Nicaea.'"

Historian Paul Maier

5. Of the examples of extrabiblical writings given in this session, which ones do you consider to be the most interesting, credible, or compelling? Elaborate.

6. Read the "Fast Fact" definition of "corroborate" on page 39 once again. In your opinion, how much of the New Testament version of the life and death of Christ has been corroborated by other sources? To what extent has the information presented and discussed in this session influenced your opinion of the biblical writings? What questions or concerns remain for you?

Optional Discussion Questions

• How much of the related chapters in *The Case for Christ* were you able to read? In what ways have these chapters influenced your opinion of the historicity and existence of Jesus Christ?

• How do you evaluate and critique one biographer from another? For instance, there have been many biographers of Abraham Lincoln: Carl Sandburg, Gore Vidal, David Herbert Donald, Stephen B. Oates, and even a documentary by Ken Burns on the Biography channel.

What are some factors that help you discern the credibility of each biography?

• What do the corroborative writings offered in this session confirm for you? What do they fail to confirm? In your opinion, which parts of Jesus' life and ministry have been corroborated?

• Some skeptics will accept material about Jesus only if it's from sources *outside* the Bible. Does that make sense to you if the biblical Gospels are rooted in eyewitness testimony? What do you think of this comment from Christian apologist Mark Mittelberg: "Why should the New Testament be ignored as a source for Jesus when it passes the tests of historicity? Just because certain documents are included in the Bible shouldn't automatically exclude them from consideration as if they are somehow tainted."

WATCH THIS!

DVD Teaching Segment #2

"When people begin religious movements, it's often not until many generations later that people record things about them, but the fact is that we have better historical documentation for Jesus than for the founder of any other ancient religion."
Historian Edwin M. Yamauchi

DISCUSS THIS!

7. Examine the following chart that compares some of the teachings in the most popular Gnostic text, the Gospel of Thomas, to the teachings of the New Testament. Do you see any way the teachings of Thomas can be reconciled with the biblical teachings? Why or why not?

Subject	Gospel of Thomas (written between 100–500 AD)	New Testament (written between 50–90 AD)
Who is Jesus?	Someone who imparts secret teachings to the disciples who are mature enough to receive it.	The redeemer who saves anyone who believes from sin (John 3:16).
Salvation	Salvation comes through a special, secret knowledge. You have to be worthy to receive that knowledge.	Salvation comes through faith in Jesus. "And you can't take credit for this; it is a gift from God" (Ephesians 2:8 NLT).
Fasting, prayer, and giving	"If you fast, you will bring sin upon yourselves, and if you pray, you will be condemned, and if you give to charity, you will harm your spirits." (Saying 14)	"When you fast, comb your hair and wash your face" (Matthew 6:17 NLT). "And pray in the Spirit on all occasions with all kinds of prayers and requests" (Ephesians 6:18 NIV). If [your gift] is contributing to the needs of others …, give generously (Romans 12:8 NIV).

"Everyone who will make herself male will enter the kingdom of heaven."
The Gospel of Thomas

Think About This!

"The various Gnostic gospels were late arrivals, which is one reason why church leaders rejected them.... They lacked authority since their authors were neither (a) apostles of Jesus nor (b) persons associated with apostles of Jesus.... No one really knows who wrote the texts."

Christian apologist Richard Abanes

8. The various Gnostic gospels were written sometime between the late second century and the sixth century AD, while even the most skeptical scholars concede the biblical Gospels were written in the first century, which is when Jesus lived. [Jesus was executed in either AD 30 or 33. Many experts date the gospel of Mark to the late 50s or early 60s; the gospels of Matthew and Luke to the early 60s; and John to the 90s (though some argue it was written earlier).] What does the dating of a gospel tell you regarding its credibility? How important is it to you that an ancient document was written close to the events it describes? How significant is it that the biblical Gospels were authored by actual apostles of Jesus or persons associated with his apostles, while the Gnostic gospels were not?

"The Bible is a product of man, my dear. Not of God.... Man created it as a historical record of tumultuous times, and it has evolved through countless translations, additions, and revisions. History has never had a definitive version of the book."

Line from the novel *The Da Vinci Code*

Think About This!

"More than eighty gospels were considered for the New Testament, and yet only a relative few were chosen for inclusion—Matthew, Mark, Luke, and John among them.... Teabing located a huge book and pulled it toward him across the table. The leather-bound edition was poster-sized, like a huge atlas. The cover read: The Gnostic Gospels. Teabing heaved it open.... 'These are photocopies of...the earliest Christian records. Troublingly, they do not match up with the gospels in the Bible....' Flipping toward the middle of the book, Teabing pointed to a passage, 'The Gospel of Philip is always a good place to start.'"

Fictional character Sir Leigh Teabing, from *The Da Vinci Code*

"There is a view among some that there were all of these different competing views of Jesus Christ and the one that won out became the orthodox perspective of Christ reflected in the Gospels. All the evidence runs contrary to that."

New Testament scholar Mark Strauss

9. Why do you think alternative stories of Jesus, contrary to the New Testament, are so intriguing or attractive to some people? Which "alternative version" of Jesus do you most often hear among your friends and colleagues?

"There are no new discoveries that tell us anything new about Jesus. The Gospel of Thomas was discovered long ago, but it's only now being used to create an alternative Jesus. Some theories about the Gospel of Thomas may be new, but the gospel itself is not."

Gregory Boyd, PhD

Think About This!

"Jesus is not a symbol of anything unless he's rooted in history. The Nicene Creed doesn't say, 'We wish these things were true.' It says, 'Jesus Christ was crucified under Pontius Pilate, and the third day he rose again from the dead,' and it goes on from there. The theological truth is based on historical truth. That's the way the New Testament reads. Look at the sermon of Peter in the second chapter of Acts. He stands up and says, 'You guys are a witness of these things; they weren't done in secret.'"

Gregory Boyd, PhD

10. In *The Case for Christ*, Dr. Gregory Boyd states, "I don't want to base my life on a symbol. I want reality." What do you think he means by this statement? Do you agree or disagree with his conviction? Is it enough that Jesus is a symbol of hope, or is it important for you to be confident that his life, teachings, and resurrection are rooted in history? Why?

Think About This!

"What do these scholars have? Well, there's a brief allusion to a lost 'secret' gospel in a late-second-century letter that has unfortunately only been seen by one person and has now itself been lost. There's a third-century account of the crucifixion and resurrection that stars a talking cross and that less than a handful of scholars think predates the Gospels. There's a second-century Gnostic document, parts of which some scholars now want to date early to back up their own preconceptions. And there is a hypothetical document built on shaky assumptions that is being sliced thinner and thinner by using circular reasoning. No, I'm sorry. I don't buy it. It's far more reasonable to put my trust in the [four biblical] Gospels — which pass the tests of historical scrutiny with flying colors."

Gregory Boyd, PhD

Optional Discussion Questions

• In the DVD clip, Craig Evans makes the observation that people are free to "pick and choose" between two versions of Jesus. Someone may prefer the second-century Gnostic Jesus better, while others might like the early first-century Palestinian Jesus. Do you think "preferences" or "feelings" are a good way to decide what to believe? Why or why not?

• Often, scholars are accused of finding the Jesus they wanted to find. Said Charlotte Allen in *The Human Christ*: "The liberal searchers found a liberal Jesus, the deists found a deist, the Romantics a Romantic, the existentialists an existentialist, and the liberationists a Jesus of class struggle." Is it possible to find the *real* Jesus? What are some ways we can safeguard against our natural tendency to make Jesus fit into our preconceptions or personal tastes?

WATCH THIS!

DVD Wrap-up/Lee's Perspective

"Just read these other documents for yourself. They're written later than the four Gospels, in the second, third, fourth, fifth, even sixth century, long after Jesus, and they're generally quite banal. They carry names — like the Gospel of Peter and the Gospel of Mary — that are unrelated to their real authorship. On the other hand, the four Gospels in the New Testament were readily accepted with remarkable unanimity as being authentic in the story they told."

Bruce Metzger, Princeton Theological Seminary

BETWEEN SESSIONS

Personal Reflection

LORD, who may dwell in your sanctuary? Who may live on your holy mountain? Those whose walk is blameless, who do what is righteous, who speak the truth from their hearts.

Psalm 15:1–2

Guide me in your truth and teach me, for you are God my Savior, and my hope is in you all day long.

Psalm 25:5

Do not withhold your mercy from me, O LORD; may your love and your truth always protect me.

Psalm 40:11 NIV

Surely you desire truth in the inner parts; you teach me wisdom in the inmost place.

Psalm 51:6 NIV

The LORD is near to all who call on him, to all who call on him in truth.

Psalm 145:18

Then you will know the truth, and the truth will set you free.

John 8:32

• What determines for you what you believe to be true? Are you a "facts and data" person or do you rely more on gut feelings? Can you think of an example of a time when a gut feeling you had proved to be true? How about a time when something you were absolutely sure of proved not to be true? How willing were you to change your mental paradigm once the facts were presented?

• What about evidence? To what extent do you genuinely examine the evidence for any given story? Are you the type that goes to *snopes.com* when a questionable email arrives? Or are you someone who considers the source of the email and lets your opinion of the sender affect your opinion of the content? Have you ever been embarrassed by forwarding information you thought was true and later found out wasn't accurate? When you discovered the correct information, how did it make you feel? Like the rest of us, you probably felt humiliated! But here is the key question: Were you glad to find out the truth or would you have preferred to continue to believe the wrong information and save yourself the humiliation? Which is most important to you: to learn the truth even when it contradicts your current belief system, or to believe in something that may be false, but is comfortable?

• How important is truth to you? According to the verses on page 51, what value do the authors of the Bible place on truth? In the last verse, Jesus is quoted as saying, "You will know the truth and the truth will set you free." What do you think Jesus meant when he said those words? What value do you think Jesus placed on the Bible? On truth? How hard are you willing to search for the truth about Jesus?

• Some would say that the story of Jesus Christ is a feel-good story that is too good to be true. Others would say there are no facts to support it and that Jesus was a mythological figure who never even existed. Many think the Bible is unreliable and the events it contains are spurious and uncorroborated by history. Is this what you have believed in the past? Is this an accurate reflection of what you believe now? Is this what the evidence supports? What have you learned in this discussion or in your reading that has challenged your current belief system? How open are you to assimilating this new information? Psalm 145:18 reads: "The LORD is near all who call on him, to all who call on him in truth." How willing are you to call on the Lord right now and disclose your beliefs, doubts, and concerns? When you do, he promises to be near you and to hear you. He is listening.

Session 4

ANALYZING JESUS

As far as I was concerned, the case was closed. There was enough proof for me to rest easy with the conclusion that the divinity of Jesus was nothing more than the fanciful invention of superstitious people.... Frankly, I had wanted to believe that the deification of Jesus was the result of legendary development in which well-meaning but misguided people slowly turned a wise sage into the mythological Son of God. That seemed safe and reassuring; after all, a roving apocalyptic preacher from the first century could make no demands on me. But while I went into my investigation thinking that this legendary explanation was intuitively obvious, I emerged convinced it was totally without basis.

Lee Strobel, *The Case for Christ*

READ THIS!

If possible, read the following content in preparation for your group meeting. Otherwise, read it as follow-up.

The Case for Christ, chapter 9: The Profile Evidence

The Case for Christ, chapter 10: The Fingerprint Evidence

WATCH THIS!

DVD Teaching Segment #1

For every DVD clip, space is provided to take notes on anything that stands out to you.

DISCUSS THIS!

1. Define "miracle." What is the difference between a miracle and a magic trick? Are real miracles possible?

"It is, therefore, at least millions to one, that the reporter of a miracle tells a lie."

Thomas Paine

2. Craig Evans points out that Jesus' contemporaries—that is, people who liked him, people who were indifferent, and people who opposed him—all acknowledged that Jesus did extraordinary things. What about you? Do you think Jesus really performed miracles such as commanding nature, healing the sick, and raising the dead? Elaborate.

"Jesus' biggest distinctive is how he did miracles on his own authority. He is the one who says, 'If I, by the finger of God, cast out demons, then the kingdom of God is among you'—he's referring to himself. He says, 'I have been anointed to set the captives free.' He does give God the Father credit for what he does, but you never find him asking God the Father to do it—he does it in the power of God the Father. And for that there is just no parallel."

Gregory Boyd, PhD

Think About This!

Now while he was in Jerusalem at the Passover Feast, many people saw the miraculous signs he was doing and believed in his name.

John 2:23 NIV

The Jews gathered around him, saying, "How long will you keep us in suspense? If you are the Christ, tell us plainly." Jesus answered, "I did tell you, but you do not believe. The miracles I do in my Father's name speak for me."

John 10:24–25 NIV

But when the Pharisees heard this, they said, "It is only by Beelzebul, the prince of demons, that this fellow drives out demons."

Matthew 12:24

3. During the time Jesus was performing miracles, people who believed in him were convinced he was filled with the Spirit of God, while those who opposed him were convinced he was of the devil. What do you think was the power source behind his miraculous acts? Elaborate. What are some factors that would delineate between a "good" power source and an "evil" power source?

Think About This!

Knowing their thoughts, Jesus said, "Why do you entertain evil thoughts in your hearts? Which is easier: to say, 'Your sins are forgiven,' or to say, 'Get up and walk'? But so that you may know that the Son of Man has authority on earth to forgive sins …" Then he said to the paralytic, "Get up, take your mat and go home."

Matthew 9:4–6 NIV

4. What do you think was the significance or ultimate purpose of Jesus' miracles?

For in Christ all the fullness of the Deity lives in bodily form.

Colossians 2:9

Think About This!

"When David sinned by committing adultery and arranging the death of the woman's husband, he ultimately says to God in Psalm 51, 'Against you only have I sinned and done this evil in your sight.' He recognized that although he had wronged people, in the end he had sinned against the God who made him in his image, and God needed to forgive him. So along comes Jesus and says to sinners, 'I forgive you.' The Jews immediately recognize the blasphemy of this. They react by saying, 'Who can forgive sins but God alone?' To my mind, that is one of the most striking things Jesus did."

New Testament scholar Donald A. Carson

5. In the DVD clip Mark Strauss suggests that the most astonishing thing Jesus did was claim to be able to forgive sins. Why is this claim so remarkable? Do you really believe Jesus has the power to forgive sins? Describe what it would feel like for you personally if you could have your slate wiped clean and every wrong you've ever done completely forgiven.

6. Strauss further explains that Jesus' miracles confirmed that he in fact did have the power and authority to forgive sins. Do you agree or disagree with Strauss's logic? Explain.

Optional Discussion Questions

- Did you have the opportunity to read the corresponding chapters from *The Case for Christ*? What impacted you most? Least? What questions or issues did this topic raise for you?

- The New Testament records at least forty separate miracles performed by Jesus. List as many of them as you can. Which one is the most outrageous? Which is the easiest to believe?

- Read the following passages recorded in Jesus' biographies. What did Jesus appear to believe about himself and his identity?

  "I and the Father are one." Again the Jews picked up stones to stone him, but Jesus said to them, "I have shown you many great miracles from the Father. For which of these do you stone me?" "We are not stoning you for any of these," replied the Jews, "but for blasphemy, because you, a mere man, claim to be God."

  John 10:30–33 NIV

  Jesus answered, "I am the way and the truth and the life. No one comes to the Father except through me. If you really know me, you will know my Father as well. From now on, you do know him and have seen him." Philip said, "Lord, show us the Father and that will be enough for us." Jesus answered: "Don't you know me, Philip, even after I have been among you such a long time? Anyone who has seen me has seen the Father. How can you say, 'Show us the Father'?"

  John 14:6–9

  Then the high priest stood up and said to Jesus, "Are you not going to answer? What is this testimony that these men are bringing against you?" But Jesus remained silent. The high priest said to him, "I charge you under oath by the living God: Tell us if you are the Christ, the Son of God." "Yes, it is as you say," Jesus replied. "But I say to all of you: In the future you will see the Son of Man sitting at the right hand of the Mighty One and coming on the clouds of heaven." Then the high priest tore his clothes and said, "He has spoken blasphemy! Why do we need any more witnesses? Look, now you have heard the blasphemy. What do you think?" "He is worthy of death," they answered.

  Matthew 26:62–66 NIV

- Which of the following attributes of Jesus would you consider to be strong evidence for his divinity?

  – He claimed to forgive sins. (Mark 2:1–12; Luke 5:17–26; 7:36–50)

– He accepted worship. (Matthew 14:33; 28:9, 17; Luke 24:52; John 9:38)

– He exorcized demons. (Matthew 8:28–34; Mark 1:34, 39; 9:14–29)

– He demonstrated control over the elements. (Matthew 8:23–27; Mark 4:35–41; John 2:1–11)

– He healed the sick. (Matthew 4:23; 8:1–13; 9:1–8, 18–34; Mark 1:34; Luke 8:40–48; John 9:1–7)

– He had authority over life and death. (Mark 5:21–43; Luke 8:49–56; John 11:1–44)

– He was said to be without sin. (1 Peter 2:22; 1 John 3:5)

- Read the following Scripture texts and quotations. Which, if any, convinces you that Jesus was the Son of Man—God in human flesh?

Again the high priest asked him, "Are you the Christ, the Son of the Blessed One?" "I am," said Jesus. "And you will see the Son of Man sitting at the right hand of the Mighty One and coming on the clouds of heaven." The high priest tore his clothes. "Why do we need any more witnesses?" he asked. "You have heard the blasphemy. What do you think?" They all condemned him as worthy of death.

Mark 14:61–64 NIV

"So look at what Jesus is doing by applying the term 'Son of Man' to himself. This is someone who approaches God himself in his heavenly throne room and is given universal authority and dominion. That makes 'Son of Man' a title of great exaltation, not of mere humanity."

Craig Blomberg, PhD

"'Son of Man' is often thought to indicate the humanity of Jesus, just as the reflex expression 'Son of God' indicates his divinity. In fact, just the opposite is true. The Son of Man was a divine figure in the Old Testament book of Daniel who would come at the end of the world to judge mankind and rule forever. Thus, the claim to be the Son of Man would be in effect a claim to divinity."

Philosopher and New Testament scholar William Lane Craig

In my vision at night I looked, and there before me was one like a son of man, coming with the clouds of heaven. He approached the Ancient of Days and was led into his presence. He was given authority, glory and sovereign power; all nations and peoples of every language worshiped him. His dominion is an everlasting dominion that will not pass away, and his kingdom is one that will never be destroyed.

Daniel 7:13–14

WATCH THIS!

DVD Teaching Segment #2

[Jesus] said to them, "This is what I told you while I was still with you: Everything must be fulfilled that is written about me in the Law of Moses, the Prophets and the Psalms."

Luke 24:44

DISCUSS THIS!

7. Where did the idea of a Messiah come from (see "Fast Fact" box below)? How and why did the Jews expect to receive a Messiah? To what degree are you looking for a Messiah in your own life?

Fast Fact

Messiah, *in Hebrew, means "the promised and expected deliverer." When the term is used in the Old Testament, it specifically pertains to the Jewish people. The Greek word for "Messiah" is "Christ." In the New Testament the Christ is revealed to be the anointed one and the deliverer who has come for all who would receive him.*

Think About This!

"The premise behind fingerprint evidence is simple: each individual has unique ridges on his or her fingers. When a print found on an object matches the pattern of ridges on a person's finger, investigators can conclude with scientific certainty that this specific individual has touched that object.... There is another kind of evidence that's analogous to fingerprints and establishes to an astounding degree of certainty that Jesus is indeed the Messiah of Israel and the world. In the Jewish Scriptures, which Christians call the Old Testament, there are several dozen major prophecies about the coming of the Messiah, who would be sent by God to redeem his people. In effect, these predictions formed a figurative fingerprint that only the Anointed One would be able to match. This way, the Israelites could rule out any impostors and validate the credentials of the authentic Messiah. The Greek word for "Messiah" is Christ. *But was Jesus really the* Christ? *Did he miraculously fulfill these predictions that were written hundreds of years before he was born? And how do we know he was the only individual throughout history who fit the prophetic fingerprint?" [See the following chart of messianic prophecies.]*

Lee Strobel

Fulfilled Prophecy	Old Testament Reference	Approximate Years Written before Jesus
He would be born of a virgin.	Isaiah 7:14	700
He would be born in Bethlehem.	Micah 5:2	700
He would be mocked and scorned, whipped, and killed by the piercing of his hands and feet. His bones would be out of joint; his garments would be divided by the casting of lots (dice).	Psalm 22	300–1,000
The time of his birth was predicted.	Daniel 9:24–26	600
He would come from the seed of a woman.	Genesis 3:15	1,400
He would be a descendant of Abraham, Isaac, Jacob, and David.	Genesis 12:3; 17:19	700–1,400
	Numbers 24:17	
	Isaiah 9:7	
He would come from the tribe of Judah.	Genesis 49:10	1,400
He would heal the deaf and blind.	Isaiah 29:18	700

He would be rejected by his own people, the Jews.	Isaiah 53:3	700
He would teach with parables.	Psalm 78:2	300–1,000
Kings and rulers would plot to kill him.	Psalm 2:2	300–1,000
He would be betrayed by a close friend.	Psalm 41:9	300–1,000
He would be betrayed for thirty pieces of silver.	Zechariah 11:12	500
His disciples would be scattered.	Zechariah 13:7	500
His bones would remain unbroken.	Psalm 34:20	300–1,000
He would be buried in a rich man's grave.	Isaiah 53:9	700
He would be resurrected on the third day.	Psalm 16:10	300–1,000
	Hosea 6:2	

8. What's your overall reaction or response to the detailed list of the messianic prophecies found in the Bible? What questions or issues does this subject matter raise in your mind?

"The Old Testament paints a portrait of God by using such titles and descriptions as Alpha and Omega, Lord, Savior, King, Judge, Light, Rock, Redeemer, Shepherd, Creator, giver of life, forgiver of sin, and speaker with divine authority. It's fascinating to note that in the New Testament each and every one is applied to Jesus. Jesus said it all in John 14:7: 'If you really knew me, you would know my Father as well.' Loose translation: 'When you look at the sketch of God from the Old Testament, you will see a likeness of me.'"

Lee Strobel

Think About This!

Consider the following words from the Jewish prophet Isaiah, written approximately seven hundred years before Jesus lived:

> He was despised and rejected by others, a man of suffering, and familiar with pain. Like one from whom people hide their faces he was despised, and we held him in low esteem. Surely he took up our pain and bore our suffering, yet we considered him punished by God, stricken by him, and afflicted. But he was pierced for our transgressions, he was crushed for our iniquities; the punishment that brought us peace was on him, and by his wounds we are healed. We all, like sheep, have gone astray, each of us has turned to our own way; and the LORD has laid on him the iniquity of us all. He was oppressed and afflicted, yet he did not open his mouth; he was led like a lamb to the slaughter, and as a sheep before its shearers is silent, so he did not open his mouth. By oppression and judgment he was taken away. Yet who of his generation protested? For he was cut off from the land of the living; for the transgression of my people he was punished. He was assigned a grave with the wicked, and with the rich in his death, though he had done no violence, nor was any deceit in his mouth.... Therefore I will give him a portion among the great, and he will divide the spoils with the strong, because he poured out his life unto death, and was numbered with the transgressors. For he bore the sin of many, and made intercession for the transgressors.
>
> Isaiah 53:3–9, 12

9. Some skeptics claim that Jesus "engineered" the fulfillment of all these prophecies. Which of the prophesies listed in the chart on pages 62–63 have some possibility of being engineered? Which would be least plausible in becoming self-fulfilling prophecies? To what extent do you think it is possible that Jesus somehow intentionally orchestrated the events of his life in order that he might fulfill each of the predictions made about the Messiah?

Think About This!

"For a few of the prophecies, yes, that's certainly conceivable that Jesus could have intentionally fulfilled them, as some claim. But there are many others for which this just wouldn't have been possible. For instance, how would he control the fact that the Sanhedrin offered Judas thirty pieces of silver to betray him? How could he arrange for his ancestry, or to be born when and where he was, or his method of execution, or that soldiers gambled for his clothing, or that his legs remained unbroken on the cross? How would he arrange to perform miracles in front of skeptics? How would he arrange for his resurrection? When you interpret Daniel 9:24–26, it foretells that the Messiah would appear a certain length of time after King Artaxerxes issued a decree for the Jewish people to go from Persia to rebuild the walls in Jerusalem. That puts the anticipated appearance of the Messiah at the exact moment in history when Jesus showed up. Certainly that's nothing he could have prearranged."

Prophecy scholar Louis Lapides

10. How does the fulfillment of the Old Testament prophecies by Jesus — and Jesus alone — relate to his identity, namely his divinity?

"[In Isaiah 53] it's almost as if God said, 'I want to make it so absolutely clear Yeshua [Jesus] is the Messiah that it's undeniable. I almost feel as if God would have to apologize to the human race and to the Jewish people for putting this passage into the Scriptures when it so clearly points to Yeshua if he didn't really mean that."

Prophecy scholar Michael L. Brown

Think About This!

"A college professor of mathematics and science named Dr. Peter Stoner wanted to determine what the odds were that any human being throughout human history could fulfill the messianic prophecies. He estimated that the odds of any human being fulfilling 48 of these ancient prophecies would be one chance in a trillion, trillion, trillion, trillion, trillion, trillion, trillion, trillion, trillion, trillion, trillion, trillion, trillion."

Lee Strobel

"I think it would be mathematically impossible for anyone else ever to fulfill all these parameters of prophecy in the Old Testament any better than Jesus did."

Ancient historian Paul Maier, Western Michigan University

"All the evidence points to Jesus as the divinely appointed fulfillment of the messianic prophecies. He was God's man, confirmed by God's signs."

Scholar Norman Geisler

"Jesus is the right continuation of my Jewish roots. He's the Messiah of Israel and the savior of the world.... So really he is the ultimate expression of God to the human race. That's why I'm spending my life talking to Jewish people—as compassionately and accurately as I can—about the reality of Jesus the Messiah. I just can't withhold God's very best from those he dearly loves."

Prophecy scholar Michael L. Brown

11. Jesus turned to his closest disciples and asked, "Who do you say I am?" To which Peter replied, "The Christ of God" (Luke 9:20 NIV). What do you imagine would have been the other disciples' reaction to Peter's declaration? What is your reaction to Peter's response? Do you think he really meant what he said? If so, what do you think convinced him?

12. How convinced are you that Jesus—and Jesus alone—fulfills the Old Testament prophecies for the Messiah? What are the implications for all of humanity if Jesus really was God in the flesh? What are the implications for *your* life if Jesus really was God in the flesh? What is a difficult or troublesome aspect of this truth for your life today?

Optional Discussion Questions

- What would prevent you from accepting the following challenge from Jewish believer in Jesus, Louis Lapides? What would motivate or inspire you to wholeheartedly accept his challenge?

  Here's my challenge to skeptics: don't accept my word for it, but don't accept your rabbi's either. Spend the time to research it yourself. Today nobody can say, "There's no information." There are plenty of books out there to help you. And one more thing: sincerely ask God to show you whether or not Jesus is the Messiah. That's what I did—and without any coaching it became clear to me who fit the fingerprint of the Messiah.

- Consider Psalm 22:1, 6–8, 16–18 (NIV) below, written hundreds of years before Jesus lived. What conclusions could you draw about the character or sanity of Jesus if he intentionally deceived people into believing he fulfilled these predictions of the Messiah if he in fact knew he was *not* really the Messiah?

  My God, my God, why have you forsaken me?… scorned by men and despised by the people. All who see me mock me; they hurl insults, shaking their heads: "He trusts in the LORD; let the LORD rescue him. Let him deliver him."… Dogs have surrounded me; a band of evil men has encircled me, they have pierced my hands and my feet. I can count all my bones; people stare and gloat over me. They divide my garments among them and cast lots for my clothing.

- To what extent has the information presented and discussed in this session influenced your opinion of the identity of Jesus Christ? What aspect of Jesus' divinity is troublesome or difficult for you to accept? Why? How convinced are you that Jesus is the Messiah, the Christ, the Anointed One, the One sent by God to be the Savior of Israel and the world? Explain.

- Is there anything in your life that would make it difficult for you to become a Christian? What anxieties do you have about believing that Jesus is the Messiah or Christ? How would your friends and family members react? Do you see any costs that you might incur if you were to become a Christian? How might those costs compare with the benefits?

WATCH THIS!

DVD Wrap-up/Lee's Perspective

"The Jews are God's chosen people, but it's important to understand that when God chose Abraham and his descendants, there was a divine purpose. It was not just to have a separated people who would be loyal to him: it was so that through Israel the entire world would be blessed and come to know the one true God."

Michael L. Brown

BETWEEN SESSIONS

Personal Reflection

Now one of the Pharisees invited Jesus to have dinner with him, so he went to the Pharisee's house and reclined at the table. When a woman who had lived a sinful life in that town learned that Jesus was eating at the Pharisee's house, she brought an alabaster jar of perfume, and as she stood behind him at his feet weeping, she began to wet his feet with her tears. Then she wiped them with her hair, kissed them and poured perfume on them.

When the Pharisee who had invited him saw this, he said to himself, "If this man were a prophet, he would know who is touching him and what kind of woman she is — that she is a sinner." Jesus answered him, "Simon, I have something to tell you." "Tell me, teacher," he said.

"Two men owed money to a certain moneylender. One owed him five hundred denarii, and the other fifty. Neither of them had the money to pay him back, so he canceled the debts of both. Now which of them will love him more?" Simon replied, "I suppose the one who had the bigger debt canceled." "You have judged correctly," Jesus said.

Then he turned toward the woman and said to Simon, "Do you see this woman? I came into your house. You did not give me any water for my feet, but she wet my feet with her tears and wiped them with her hair. You did not give me a kiss, but this woman, from the time I entered, has not stopped kissing my feet. You did not put oil on my head, but she has poured perfume on my feet. Therefore, I tell you, her many sins have been forgiven — for she loved much. But he who has been forgiven little loves little." Then Jesus said to her, "Your sins are forgiven." The other guests began to say among themselves, "Who is this who even forgives sins?" Jesus said to the woman, "Your faith has saved you; go in peace."

Luke 7:36-50 NIV

- Do you believe in God? Do you believe Jesus is the Son of Man, the Messiah, the promised deliverer? Think about your own sins and shortfalls. Think about the most shameful things you have ever done. Remember the lies, the cheating, the stealing, the lusting ... what about the selfish times, and putting things or people before God?

- When Jesus walked this earth, he claimed to be able to forgive even the worst sins of all those who repented and had faith in him. In his death he paid the price for the sins of all humankind — including yours. Think about your sin and then consider the sins of all of humanity throughout history. Can a mere human being actually forgive everything you have ever done wrong, much less take the punishment for the sins of all humankind? This is what Jesus claimed to do. What do you make of Jesus' claims? If Jesus is divine and has the authority to forgive sin, what does this mean for you personally? How miraculous would it be for you to have your lifetime's accumulation of mistakes and failures completely forgiven and forever forgotten?

• Consider the woman in the account from Luke 7. Do you think she was any more or less sinful than you have been? How did she respond to Jesus? Contrast the Pharisee's attitude toward her with Jesus' attitude toward her. Jesus tells us that she loved much because she had been forgiven much. What do you think led her to worship and love Jesus as she did? Is there anything that could lead you to love him with such abandon?

• The Bible teaches that if we confess, repent (turn away from our sin), and ask for forgiveness, we will be totally forgiven and received into the family of God. Have you ever considered asking for God's forgiveness? Have you ever considered casting all of your sins upon Jesus, who has offered to take them from you and absolve you of all wrongdoing? You can ask this of Christ anywhere at any time with a simple, heartfelt prayer. When you turn to him in genuine faith, he promises that absolutely nothing will keep him from coming to you. He himself said, "Come to me, all you who are weary and burdened, and I will give you rest. Take my yoke upon you and learn from me, for I am gentle and humble in heart, and you will find rest for your souls" (Matthew 11:28–29).

EVIDENCE
FOR THE RESURRECTION

Occasionally bodies turn up missing in pulp fiction and real life, but rarely do you encounter an empty tomb.... The issue with Jesus isn't that he was nowhere to be seen. It's that he was seen, alive; he was seen, dead; and he was seen, alive once more. If we believe the Gospel accounts, this isn't a matter of a missing body. No, it's a matter of Jesus still being alive, even to this day, even after publicly succumbing to the horrors of crucifixion.

Lee Strobel, *The Case for Christ*

READ THIS!

If possible, read the following content in preparation for your group meeting. Otherwise, read it as follow-up.

The Case for Christ, chapter 11: The Medical Evidence

The Case for Christ, chapter 12: The Evidence of the Missing Body

The Case for Christ, chapter 13: The Evidence of Appearances

WATCH THIS!

DVD Teaching Segment #1

For every DVD clip, space is provided to take notes on anything that stands out to you.

DISCUSS THIS!

1. Do you agree that, if true, the resurrection of Jesus is the pivotal event of history? Why or why not?

"Clearly, the weight of the historical and medical evidence indicates that Jesus was dead before the wound to his side was inflicted.... Accordingly, interpretations based on the assumption that Jesus did not die on the cross appear to be at odds with modern medical knowledge."

William D. Edwards, 1986 article in the *Journal of the American Medical Association*

2. Consider the following deduction: *If it can be shown that Jesus really did return from the dead, then it can be concluded that Jesus really is who he claimed to be: the one and only Son of God.* Do you agree or disagree? Would verification of the resurrection convince you of Jesus' divinity? Explain.

3. Some skeptics claim that although Jesus might have been crucified, he never really died. Instead, he merely fainted on the cross or was drugged, and later escaped as part of a conspiracy. To what extent do you think the "swoon hypothesis" outlined on page 74 makes sense? Give reasons for your explanation.

"The pain was absolutely unbearable. In fact, it was literally beyond words to describe; they had to invent a new word: excruciating. *Literally,* excruciating *means 'out of the cross.' Think of that: they needed to create a new word, because there was nothing in the language that could describe the intense anguish caused during the crucifixion."*

Alexander Metherell, MD, PhD

Think About This!

The Swoon Hypothesis

The idea that Jesus never really died on the cross can be found in the Koran, which was written in the seventh century — in fact, Ahmadiya Muslims contend that Jesus actually fled to India. To this day there's a shrine that allegedly marks his real burial place in Srinagar, Kashmir.

As the nineteenth century dawned, Karl Bahrdt, Karl Venturini, and others tried to explain away the resurrection by suggesting that Jesus only fainted from exhaustion on the cross, or he had been given a drug that made him appear to die, and that he had later been revived by the cool, damp air of the tomb.

Conspiracy theorists bolstered this hypothesis by pointing out that Jesus had been given some liquid on a sponge while on the cross (Mark 15:36) and that Pilate seemed surprised at how quickly Jesus had succumbed (Mark 15:44). Consequently, they said, Jesus' reappearance wasn't a miraculous resurrection but merely a fortuitous resuscitation, and his tomb was empty because he continued to live.

Like an urban myth, the swoon theory continues to flourish. But what does the evidence really establish? What actually happened at the crucifixion? What was Jesus' cause of death? Is there any possible way he could have survived this ordeal?

4. Read the following sections (pages 75 – 77) outlining some of the medical evidence behind a Roman crucifixion. How might medical analysis today shed light on the death of Jesus two thousand years ago? What questions or issues do you have regarding the death of Jesus?

Think About This!

Medical Evidence

Medical evidence can be crucial. It can determine whether a child died of abuse or an accidental fall. It can establish whether a person succumbed to natural causes or was murdered by someone who spiked the person's coffee with arsenic. It can uphold or dismantle a defendant's alibi by pinpointing the victim's time of death, using an ingenious procedure that measures the amount of potassium in the eyes of the deceased. And yes, even in the case of someone brutally executed on a Roman cross two millennia ago, medical evidence can still make a crucial contribution: it can destroy one of the most persistent arguments used by those who claim that the resurrection of Jesus — the supreme vindication of his claim to deity — was nothing more than an elaborate hoax.

Jesus Is Flogged

Then Pilate took Jesus and had him flogged. The soldiers twisted together a crown of thorns and put it on his head. They clothed him in a purple robe and went up to him again and again, saying, "Hail, king of the Jews!" And they slapped him in the face.

John 19:1-3

Then the governor's soldiers took Jesus into the Praetorium and gathered the whole company of soldiers around him. They stripped him and put a scarlet robe on him, and then twisted together a crown of thorns and set it on his head. They put a staff in his right hand as a scepter. Then they knelt in front of him and mocked him. "Hail, king of the Jews!" they said. They spit on him, and took the staff and struck him on the head again and again. After they had mocked him, they took off the robe and put his own clothes on him. Then they led him away to crucify him.

Matthew 27:27-31

Roman Floggings

"Roman floggings were known to be terribly brutal. They usually consisted of thirty-nine lashes. The soldier would use a whip of braided leather thongs with metal balls woven into them. When the whip would strike the flesh, these balls would cause deep bruises or contusions, which would break open with further blows. And the whip had pieces of sharp bone as well, which would cut the flesh severely. One physician who has studied Roman beatings said, 'As the flogging

continued, the lacerations would tear into the underlying skeletal muscles and produce quivering ribbons of bleeding flesh.' A third-century historian by the name of Eusebius described a flogging by saying, 'The sufferer's veins were laid bare, and the very muscles, sinews, and bowels of the victim were open to exposure.' We know that many people would die from this kind of beating even before they could be crucified. At the least, the victim would experience tremendous pain and go into hypovolemic shock."

Alexander Metherell, MD, PhD

Fast Fact

Hypovolemic shock: Hypo means "low," vol refers to volume, and emic means "blood," so hypovolemic shock means the person is suffering the effects of losing a large amount of blood. This does four things. First, the heart races to try to pump blood that isn't there; second, the blood pressure drops, causing fainting or collapse; third, the kidneys stop producing urine to maintain what volume is left; and fourth, the person becomes very thirsty as the body craves fluids to replace the lost blood volume.

Think About This!

Jesus Is Crucified

So the soldiers took charge of Jesus. Carrying his own cross, he went out to the place of the Skull (which in Aramaic is called Golgotha). Here they crucified him, and with him two others—one on each side and Jesus in the middle. Pilate had a notice prepared and fastened to the cross. It read: JESUS OF NAZARETH, THE KING OF THE JEWS. Many of the Jews read this sign, for the place where Jesus was crucified was near the city, and the sign was written in Aramaic, Latin and Greek. The chief priests of the Jews protested to Pilate, "Do not write 'The King of the Jews,' but that this man claimed to be king of the Jews." Pilate answered, "What I have written, I have written." When the soldiers crucified Jesus, they took his clothes, dividing them into four shares, one for each of them, with the undergarment remaining. This garment was seamless, woven in one piece from top to bottom. "Let's not tear it," they said to one another. "Let's decide by lot who will get it." This happened that the scripture might be fulfilled that said, "They *divided my clothes among them and cast lots for my garment." So this is what the soldiers did.*

John 19:16b–24

Those who passed by hurled insults at him, shaking their heads and saying, "So! You who are going to destroy the temple and build it in three days, come down from the cross and save yourself!" In the same way the chief priests and the teachers of the law mocked him among themselves. "He saved others," they said, "but he can't save himself! Let this Messiah, this King of Israel, come down now from the cross, that we may see and believe." Those crucified with him also heaped insults on him.

Mark 15:29–32

Later, knowing that everything had now been finished, and so that Scripture would be fulfilled, Jesus said, "I am thirsty." A jar of wine vinegar was there, so they soaked a sponge in it, put the sponge on a stalk of the hyssop plant, and lifted it to Jesus' lips. When he had received the drink, Jesus said, "It is finished." With that, he bowed his head and gave up his spirit.

John 19:28–30

Death by Asphyxiation

"Once a person is hanging in the vertical position, crucifixion is essentially an agonizingly slow death by asphyxiation. The reason is that the stresses on the muscles and diaphragm put the chest into the inhaled position; basically, in order to exhale, the individual must push up on his feet so the tension on the muscles would be eased for a moment. In doing so, the nail would tear through the foot, eventually locking up against the tarsal bones. After managing to exhale, the person would then be able to relax down and take another breath in. Again he'd have to push himself up to exhale, scraping his bloodied back against the coarse wood of the cross. This would go on and on until complete exhaustion would take over, and the person wouldn't be able to push up and breathe anymore."

Alexander Metherell

5. Which piece of medical evidence most stands out to you as substantiating evidence for the biblical account of the crucifixion and death of Jesus? Which is the weakest piece of evidence or makes the least amount of sense? In your opinion, what are the odds that Jesus really survived his crucifixion? Do you think it's possible that Jesus didn't actually die on the cross and his "resurrection" was only a "near death" experience from which he recovered? Give reasons for your answers.

Think About This!

Jesus Sweats Blood

Jesus went out as usual to the Mount of Olives, and his disciples followed him. On reaching the place, he said to them, "Pray that you will not fall into temptation." He withdrew about a stone's throw beyond them, knelt down and prayed, "Father, if you are willing, take this cup from me; yet not my will, but yours be done." An angel from heaven appeared to him and strengthened him. And being in anguish, he prayed more earnestly, and his sweat was like drops of blood falling to the ground.

Luke 22:39 – 44

Fast Fact

Hematidrosis: *"[Hematidrosis] not very common, but it is associated with a high degree of psychological stress. What happens is that severe anxiety causes the release of chemicals that break down the capillaries in the sweat glands. As a result, there's a small amount of bleeding into these glands, and the sweat comes out tinged with blood. We're not talking about a lot of blood; it's just a very, very small amount."*

Alexander Metherell

Think About This!

Pierced but Not Broken

Now it was the day of Preparation, and the next day was to be a special Sabbath. Because the Jewish leaders did not want the bodies left on the crosses during the Sabbath, they asked Pilate to have the legs broken and the bodies taken down. The soldiers therefore came and broke the legs of the first man who had been crucified with Jesus, and then those of the other. But when they came to Jesus and found that he was already dead, they did not break his legs. Instead, one of the soldiers pierced Jesus' side with a spear, bringing a sudden flow of blood and water. The man who saw it has given testimony, and his testimony is true. He knows that he tells the truth, and he testifies so that you also may believe. These things happened so that the scripture would be fulfilled: "Not one of his bones will be broken," and, as another scripture says, "They will look on the one they have pierced."

John 19:31–37

Fast Fact

Pericardial and pleural effusion: *"Even before he died — and this is important, too — the hypovolemic shock would have caused a sustained rapid heart rate that would have contributed to heart failure, resulting in the collection of fluid in the membrane around the heart, called a pericardial effusion, as well as around the lungs, which is called a pleural effusion.... [T]he Roman soldier came around and, being fairly certain that Jesus was dead, confirmed it by thrusting a spear into his right side. The spear apparently went through the right lung and into the heart, so when the spear was pulled out, some fluid — the pericardial effusion and the pleural effusion — came out. This would have the appearance of a clear fluid, like water, followed by a large volume of blood, as the eyewitness John described in his Gospel. John probably had no idea why he saw both blood and a clear fluid come out — certainly that's not what an untrained person like him would have anticipated. Yet John's description is consistent with what modern medicine would expect to have happened. I'll grant you that the soldiers didn't go to medical school. But remember that they were experts in killing people — that was their job, and they did it very well. They knew without a doubt when a person was dead, and really it's not so terribly* *difficult to figure out. Besides, if a prisoner somehow escaped, the responsible soldiers would be put to death themselves, so they had a huge incentive to make absolutely sure that each and every victim was dead when he was removed from the cross."*

Alexander Metherell

6. Did you know that Jesus was so anguished in the garden that his sweat became like drops of blood? (See "Think About This!" and "Fast Fact" box on page 78.) How surprised are you to learn that blood in the sweat glands is an actual medical condition due to high levels of stress? How does this medical fact affect the credibility of the biblical account? What do you think was the cause of Jesus' anguish and stress in the garden?

7. In John's account of the death of Jesus, he gives a seemingly irrelevant, secondary detail that when the soldier pierced Jesus' side to be sure he was dead, both water and blood came out. (See "Think About This!" and "Fast Fact" box on pages 79–80.) Given that there was no medical knowledge of the conditions known as pericardial effusion (water around the heart) or pleural effusion (water around the lungs) at that time, what significance does this detail add to the credibility and accuracy of John's account?

Optional Discussion Questions

• How much of the related chapters in *The Case for Christ* did you have an opportunity to read? Was there any information from the book that impacted you one way or the other regarding the evidence surrounding Jesus' crucifixion and death? Which were the least and most convincing arguments for the case for Christ? What additional questions remain in your mind?

• How does the Bible's prediction that during the crucifixion Jesus' body would be pierced but his bones left unbroken impact your view of his divinity?

• Given the severity of the penalty for an escaped prisoner during the Roman era, how motivated were the guards to prevent such an occurrence? How does this fact affect the credibility of the biblical account surrounding Jesus' death and resurrection?

WATCH THIS!

DVD Teaching Segment #2

"The chances of surviving the crucifixion were extremely bleak. Crucifixion and the tortures that normally preceded it was the worse way to die in antiquity. A person was scourged to the point usually that their intestines, arteries and veins were laid bare. And then after that a person was dragged out where they were impaled to a cross or a tree. And then left hanging there in excruciating pain."

Resurrection expert Michael Licona

DISCUSS THIS!

8. Read the section starting below about the burial of Jesus. What issues does it raise for you? How convinced are you that Jesus' body was securely buried in the tomb after his death?

"The empty tomb ... is the ultimate representation of Jesus' claim to being God."

Lee Strobel

Think About This!

The Burial

As evening approached, there came a rich man from Arimathea, named Joseph, who had himself become a disciple of Jesus. Going to Pilate, he asked for Jesus' body, and Pilate ordered that it be given to him. Joseph took the body, wrapped it in a clean linen cloth, and placed it in his own new tomb that he had cut out of the rock. He rolled a big stone in front of the entrance to the tomb and went away. Mary Magdalene and the other Mary were sitting there opposite the tomb. The next day, the one after Preparation Day, the chief priests and the Pharisees went to Pilate. "Sir," they said, "we remember that while he was still alive that deceiver said, 'After three days I will rise again.' So give the order for the tomb to be made secure until the third day. Otherwise, his disciples may come and steal the body and tell the people that he has been raised from the dead. This last deception will be worse than the first." "Take a guard," Pilate answered. "Go, make the tomb as secure as you know how." So they went and made the tomb secure by putting a seal on the stone and posting the guard.

Matthew 27:57–66

The Tomb

"There was a slanted groove that led down to a low entrance, and a large disk-shaped stone was rolled down this groove and lodged into place across the door. A smaller stone was then used to secure the disk. Although it would be easy to roll this big disk down the groove, it would take several men to roll the stone back up in order to reopen the tomb. In that sense it was quite secure."

William Lane Craig

9. Read the account on page 84 of the discovery of the empty tomb. What questions does it raise or answer for you? Some skeptics suggest that if Jesus was really dead and buried, then the idea of an empty tomb is impossible. So they conclude that either Jesus never really died or the tomb was never found empty. What do you think? Was the tomb really found empty? Why or why not?

"When we turn to the Gospels, we find multiple, independent attestation of this burial story, and Joseph of Arimathea is specifically named in all four accounts. On top of that, the burial story in Mark is so extremely early that it's simply not possible for it to have been subject to legendary corruption. When you read the New Testament, there's no doubt that the disciples sincerely believed the truth of the resurrection, which they proclaimed to their deaths. The idea that the empty tomb is the result of some hoax, conspiracy, or theft is simply dismissed today."

William Lane Craig

Think About This!

The Empty Tomb

After the Sabbath, at dawn on the first day of the week, Mary Magdalene and the other Mary went to look at the tomb. There was a violent earthquake, for an angel of the Lord came down from heaven and, going to the tomb, rolled back the stone and sat on it. His appearance was like lightning, and his clothes were white as snow. The guards were so afraid of him that they shook and became like dead men.

The angel said to the women, "Do not be afraid, for I know that you are looking for Jesus, who was crucified. He is not here; he has risen, just as he said. Come and see the place where he lay. Then go quickly and tell his disciples: 'He has risen from the dead and is going ahead of you into Galilee. There you will see him.' Now I have told you."

So the women hurried away from the tomb, afraid yet filled with joy, and ran to tell his disciples. Suddenly Jesus met them. "Greetings," he said. They came to him, clasped his feet and worshiped him. Then Jesus said to them, "Do not be afraid. Go and tell my brothers to go to Galilee; there they will see me."

While the women were on their way, some of the guards went into the city and reported to the chief priests everything that had happened. When the chief priests had met with the elders and devised a plan, they gave the soldiers a large sum of money, telling them, "You are to say, 'His disciples came during the night and stole him away while we were asleep.' If this report gets to the governor, we will satisfy him and keep you out of trouble." So the soldiers took the money and did as they were instructed. And this story has been widely circulated among the Jews to this very day.

Matthew 28:1–15

10. William Lane Craig, N. T. Wright, and Michael Licona contend that if the empty tomb story were fabricated by Jesus' disciples, they never would have had said that its discovery was made by women, due to women's low status in that day. Does this argument make sense to you? Do you agree with it? Why or why not?

Think About This!

"When you understand the role of women in first-century Jewish society, what's really extraordinary is that this empty tomb story should feature women as the discoverers of the empty tomb in the first place. Women were on a very low rung of the social ladder in first-century Palestine. There are old rabbinical sayings that said, 'Let the words of the Law be burned rather than delivered to women' and 'Blessed is he whose children are male, but woe to him whose children are female.' In light of this, it's absolutely remarkable that the chief witnesses to the empty tomb are these women who were friends of Jesus. Any later legendary account would have certainly portrayed male disciples as discovering the tomb — Peter or John, for example. The fact that women are the first witnesses to the empty tomb is most plausibly explained by the reality that — like it or not — they were the discoverers of the empty tomb! This shows that the Gospel writers faithfully recorded what happened, even if it was embarrassing. This bespeaks the historicity of this tradition rather than its legendary status."

William Lane Craig

11. Mark Strauss and Michael Licona point out that since the Jewish authorities tried to claim that the disciples had stolen the body of Jesus, this supports the fact that the tomb was really empty. Do you agree or disagree with this logic? Why?

"True, the discovery of the empty tomb is differently described by the various Gospels, but if we apply the same sort of criteria that we would apply to any other ancient literary sources, then the evidence is firm and plausible enough to necessitate the conclusion that the tomb was, indeed, found empty."

Historian Michael Grant

Optional Discussion Questions

• Even Jesus' enemies acknowledged that the tomb was empty. What weight does this give to the credibility of this claim? Why?

• Everyone in the ancient world admitted the tomb was empty; the issue was how it got that way. Can you think of any logical explanation for the vacant tomb other than the resurrection of Jesus?

• Do you agree or disagree with the following statements? Give reasons for your responses.

 – Jesus' tomb was not really empty.

 – The disciples stole the body.

 – The women went to the wrong tomb.

 – The disciples embellished the story of the empty tomb because they were Jesus' friends.

 – The empty tomb was simply a legend that developed over time.

• What's your own conclusion concerning whether Jesus' tomb was found empty on Easter morning? What evidence did you find most convincing in coming to that judgment?

WATCH THIS!

DVD Teaching Segment #3

DISCUSS THIS!

12. If Jesus did, in fact, die on a cross, and the tomb in which he was buried was really found to be empty, what happened to Jesus? Do you believe Jesus was resurrected? Give reasons for what you believe.

> *"I know pretty well what evidence is, and I tell you, such evidence as that for the resurrection has never broken down yet."*
> John Singleton Copley, one of the greatest legal minds in British history

Think About This!

Jesus Is Risen

Now Mary stood outside the tomb crying. As she wept, she bent over to look into the tomb and saw two angels in white, seated where Jesus' body had been, one at the head and the other at the foot. They asked her, "Woman, why are you crying?" "They have taken my Lord away," she said, "and I don't know where they have put him." At this, she turned around and saw Jesus standing there, but she did not realize that it was Jesus. He asked her, "Woman, why are you crying? Who is it you are looking for?" Thinking he was the gardener, she said, "Sir, if you have carried him away, tell me where you have put him, and I will get him." Jesus said to her, "Mary." She turned toward him and cried out in Aramaic, "Rabboni!" (which means "Teacher"). Jesus said, "Do not hold on to me, for I have not yet ascended to the Father. Go instead to my brothers and tell them, 'I am ascending to my Father and your Father, to my God and your God.'" Mary Magdalene went to the disciples with the news: "I have seen the Lord!" And she told them that he had said these things to her.

John 20:11–18

> *"The appearances of Jesus are as well authenticated as anything in antiquity.... There can be no rational doubt that they occurred, and that the main reason why Christians became sure of the resurrection in the earliest days was just this. They could say with assurance, 'We have seen the Lord.' They knew it was he."*
>
> British theologian Michael Green

13. Do you believe that people really witnessed Jesus alive after the crucifixion? Why or why not? What is difficult to accept about Jesus' post-resurrection appearances?

> *"It was therefore impossible that they [the early Christians] could have persisted in affirming the truths they have narrated, had not Jesus actually risen from the dead, and had they not known this fact as certainly as they knew any other fact."*
>
> Simon Greenleaf, an authority in jurisprudence at Harvard Law School

Think About This!

The Earliest Christian Creed

For what I received I passed on to you as of first importance: that Christ died for our sins according to the Scriptures, that he was buried, that he was raised on the third day according to the Scriptures, and that he appeared to Cephas [Peter], and then to the Twelve. After that, he appeared to more than five hundred of the brothers and sisters at the same time, most of whom are still living, though some have fallen asleep. Then he appeared to James, then to all the apostles.

1 Corinthians 15:3–7

14. The creed in 1 Corinthians 15 is the only place in ancient literature where it is claimed that Jesus appeared to five hundred people at once. The Gospels don't mention it. No secular historian mentions it. Study the section below. Do you agree with the reasons historian Gary Habermas gives that this creed is the earliest and one of the best authenticated passages in Scripture? Why or why not?

Think About This!

"We know that Paul wrote 1 Corinthians between AD 55 and 57. He indicates in 1 Corinthians 15:1–4 that he has already passed on this creed to the church at Corinth, which would mean it must predate his visit there in AD 51. Therefore the creed was being used within twenty years of the resurrection, which is quite early. However, I'd agree with the various scholars who trace it back even further, to within two to eight years of the resurrection, or from about AD 32 to 38, when Paul received it in either Damascus or Jerusalem. So this is incredibly early material—primitive, unadorned testimony to the fact that Jesus appeared alive to skeptics like Paul and James, as well as to Peter and the rest of the disciples.

"Now, stop and think about it: you would never include this phrase [the 500] unless you were absolutely confident that these folks would confirm that they really did see Jesus alive. I mean, Paul was virtually inviting people to check it out for themselves! He wouldn't have said this if he didn't know they'd back him up. Look, I'd love to have five sources for this. I don't. But I do have one excellent source—a creed that's so good that German historian Hans von Campenhausen says, 'This account meets all the demands of historical reliability that could possibly be made of such a text.' The creed is early ... it's free from legendary contamination, ... it's unambiguous and specific, and ... it's ultimately rooted in eyewitness accounts."

Gary Habermas, PhD

15. What is your own conclusion regarding the validity of the 1 Corinthians 15 creed? How pivotal is this creed to your assessment of whether Jesus was seen alive after the crucifixion?

Think About This!

The Appearances

When they had carried out all that was written about him, they took him down from the tree and laid him in a tomb. But God raised him from the dead, and for many days he was seen by those who had traveled with him from Galilee to Jerusalem. They are now his witnesses to our people.

Acts 13:29-31

"Without having a reliable testimony for the emptiness of Jesus' tomb, the early Christian community could not have survived in Jerusalem proclaiming the resurrection of Christ."

German scholar Wolfhart Pannenberg

Early in the morning, Jesus stood on the shore, but the disciples did not realize that it was Jesus. He called out to them, "Friends, haven't you any fish?" "No," they answered. He said, "Throw your net on the right side of the boat and you will find some." When they did, they were unable to haul the net in because of the large number of fish. Then the disciple whom Jesus loved said to Peter, "It is the Lord!" As soon as Simon Peter heard him say, "It is the Lord," he wrapped his outer garment around him (for he had taken it off) and jumped into the water. The other disciples followed in the boat, towing the net full of fish, for they were not far from shore, about a hundred yards. When they landed, they saw a fire of burning coals there with fish on it, and some bread. Jesus said to them, "Bring some of the fish you have just caught." Simon Peter climbed aboard and dragged the net ashore. It was full of large fish, 153, but even with so many the net was not torn. Jesus said to them, "Come and have breakfast." None of the disciples dared ask him, "Who are you?" They knew it was the Lord. Jesus came, took the bread and gave it to them, and did the same with the fish. This was now the third time Jesus appeared to his disciples after he was raised from the dead.

John 21:4–14

"Even the more skeptical historians agree that for primitive Christianity ... the resurrection of Jesus from the dead was a real event in history, the very foundation of faith, and not a mythical idea arising out of the creative imagination of believers."

Historian Carl Braaten

16. The apostle Paul writes in 1 Corinthians 15:14: "And if Christ has not been raised, our preaching is useless and so is your faith." Why does Paul call the resurrection of Jesus the very linchpin of the Christian faith?

On the evening of that first day of the week, when the disciples were together, with the doors locked for fear of the Jewish leaders, Jesus came and stood among them and said, "Peace be with you!" After he said this, he showed them his hands and side. The disciples were overjoyed when they saw the Lord.
John 20:19–20

Optional Discussion Questions

- How feasible is it that Jesus' resurrection appearances really took place? If so, why weren't they more widely reported among those who were not Christians? If, as the early Christian creed states, five hundred people saw the resurrected Jesus at once, why don't other historians, like Josephus, report it? Is it possible that the number "500" could be symbolic or at least hyperbolic? Give reasons for your responses.

- Gary Habermas reduced the issue of the resurrection down to two questions: Did Jesus die? And, was he later seen alive? Based on the evidence so far, how would you answer those questions?

- Could there be any plausible alternatives to explain away the encounters people had with the risen Jesus? Could these accounts be legendary in nature? Or how likely is it that the witnesses had all experienced the same hallucination?

- Gary Habermas concludes in *The Case for Christ* that sometimes people grasp at straws trying to disprove Jesus' appearances, but nothing fits the evidence better than the explanation that Jesus was found alive after he was dead and buried. What do you make of this conclusion?

WATCH THIS!

DVD Wrap-up/Lee's Perspective

BETWEEN SESSIONS

Personal Reflection

On his arrival, Jesus found that Lazarus had already been in the tomb for four days. Now Bethany was less than two miles from Jerusalem, and many Jews had come to Martha and Mary to comfort them in the loss of their brother. When Martha heard that Jesus was coming, she went out to meet him, but Mary stayed at home.

"Lord," Martha said to Jesus, "if you had been here, my brother would not have died. But I know that even now God will give you whatever you ask." Jesus said to her, "Your brother will rise again." Martha answered, "I know he will rise again in the resurrection at the last day."

Jesus said to her, "I am the resurrection and the life. Anyone who believes in me will live, even though they die; and whoever lives by believing in me will never die. Do you believe this?" "Yes, Lord," she told him, "I believe that you are the Messiah, the Son of God, who was to come into the world." ...

When Mary reached the place where Jesus was and saw him, she fell at his feet and said, "Lord, if you had been here, my brother would not have died." When Jesus saw her weeping, and the Jews who had come along with her also weeping, he was deeply moved in spirit and troubled. "Where have you laid him?" he asked. "Come and see, Lord," they replied. Jesus wept....

Then Jesus looked up and said, "Father, I thank you that you have heard me. I knew that you always hear me, but I said this for the benefit of the people standing here, that they may believe that you sent me." When he had said this, Jesus called in a loud voice, "Lazarus, come out!" The dead man came out, his hands and feet wrapped with strips of linen, and a cloth around his face. Jesus said to them, "Take off the grave clothes and let him go."

John 11:17 – 27, 32 – 35, 41b – 44

- Have you ever lost someone you loved? If so, perhaps you can relate to Martha's feelings of frustration and pain upon seeing Jesus. Were you angry like she was that God didn't intervene in some way to prevent it? Like Martha, do you have a distant hope that your loved one will one day rise again? If so, what leads you to believe that there is life after death? From where does your hope come? Is it simply wishful thinking, or is your hope grounded in reality?

- Now that you've had a chance to evaluate the evidence, what have you concluded about Jesus' power and authority over death? Did Jesus really return alive from the dead? Was the resurrection a legend, a hoax, or was it an actual event that changed the history of the world? What's your own conclusion concerning whether Jesus' tomb was empty on that first Easter morning, and what does it mean for you personally?

- *The resurrection is the supreme vindication of Jesus' divine identity and his inspired teaching. It's the proof of his triumph over sin and death. It's the foreshadowing of the eternal resurrection of his followers and the basis of all Christian hope! It's the miracle of all miracles.* Do these statements make sense to you, or are they difficult for you to believe? What do you think is significant about the resurrection?

- Reread the exchange between Jesus and Martha on page 93. Claiming he was able to defeat spiritual death and impart eternal life to anyone who believes in him, Jesus asked Martha, "Do you believe this?" Imagine you are in Martha's place and Jesus is asking you the same question. "Do you believe this?" What is *your* response?

- Whether you believe, disbelieve, or are wrestling with doubts, Jesus is alive today and is willing to meet you wherever you are. Why don't you speak to him at this moment and ask him to reveal himself to you? He is waiting to give you hope and eternal life even now.

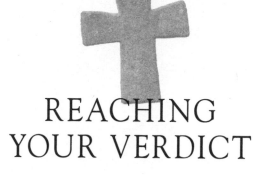

REACHING YOUR VERDICT

Having already considered the persuasive evidence for the empty tomb, and eyewitness accounts of the risen Jesus, it was time for me to seek out any circumstantial evidence that might bolster the case for the resurrection. I knew that if an event as extraordinary as the resurrection of Jesus had really occurred, history would be littered with indirect evidence backing it up.

Lee Strobel

READ THIS!

If possible, read the following content in preparation for your group meeting. Otherwise, read it as follow-up.

The Case for Christ, conclusion: The Verdict of History

WATCH THIS!

DVD Teaching Segment #1

For every DVD clip, space is provided to take notes on anything that stands out to you.

Fast Fact

Circumstantial Evidence

"*Eyewitness testimony is called direct evidence because people describe under oath how they personally saw the defendant commit the crime. While this is often compelling, it can sometimes be subject to faded memories, prejudices, and even outright fabrication. In contrast, circumstantial evidence is made up of indirect facts from which inferences can be rationally drawn. Its cumulative effect can be every bit as strong — and in many instances even more potent — than eyewitness accounts.... Circumstantial evidence is plural rather than singular. In other words, it's built brick by brick by brick until there's a sturdy foundation on which conclusions can be confidently based.*"

Lee Strobel

DISCUSS THIS!

1. What is the difference between direct evidence and circumstantial (indirect) evidence? (See "Fast Fact" box on page 96.) Give examples of each. In what ways might circumstantial evidence, such as eyewitness accounts, be just as compelling as direct evidence?

2. Do you agree that if an event as extraordinary as the resurrection of Jesus had actually occurred, history would be littered with indirect evidence backing it up? Why or why not? Can you give an example of the kind of circumstantial evidence you think would bolster the case for the resurrection? If the resurrection were a hoax, what sort of circumstantial evidence would substantiate that?

Think About This!

The Disciples Were Willing to Suffer and Die for Their Beliefs

"When Jesus was crucified his followers were discouraged and depressed. They no longer had confidence that Jesus had been sent by God, because they believed anyone crucified was accursed by God. They also had been taught that God would not let his Messiah suffer death. So they dispersed. The Jesus movement was all but stopped in its tracks. Then, after a short period of time, we see them abandoning their occupations, regathering, and committing themselves to spreading a very specific message—that Jesus Christ was the Messiah of God who died on a cross, returned to life, and was seen alive by them. And they were willing to spend the rest of their lives proclaiming this, without any payoff from a human point of view. It's not as though there were a mansion awaiting them on the Mediterranean. They faced a life of hardship. They often went without food, slept exposed to the elements, were ridiculed, beaten, imprisoned. And finally, most of them were executed in torturous ways....

"However, the apostles were willing to die for something they had seen with their own eyes and touched with their own hands. They were in a unique position not to just believe Jesus rose from the dead but to know for sure. And when you've got eleven credible people with no ulterior motives, with nothing to gain and a lot to lose, who all agree they observed something with their own eyes—now you've got some difficulty explaining that away."

J. P. Moreland, PhD

Five times I [Paul] received from the Jews the forty lashes minus one. Three times I was beaten with rods, once I was pelted with stones, three times I was shipwrecked, I spent a night and a day in the open sea, I have been constantly on the move. I have been in danger from rivers, in danger from bandits, in danger from my own people, in danger from Gentiles; in danger in the city, in danger in the country, in danger at sea; and in danger from false believers. I have labored and toiled and have often gone without sleep; I have known hunger and thirst and have often gone without food; I have been cold and naked.

2 Corinthians 11:24–27

3. When Jesus was executed, his disciples became fearful for their lives and they scattered. Their hopes had been dashed because the one they had believed to be the Messiah was murdered by crucifixion under the authority of the Roman Empire. Yet shortly thereafter, the disciples took a stand in Jerusalem proclaiming that Jesus was the Messiah, the very Son of God. What do you think accounts for the difference between the sorrowful, fearful disciples on the Friday of the crucifixion and the emboldened, fearless disciples?

4. Mark Strauss and J. P. Moreland point out that when Jesus' followers discovered that Jesus had actually defeated death, they moved from discouragement and bewilderment to great joy and renewed hope, willing to endure incredible hardships, and even die for the cause of the gospel without ever recanting their belief that Jesus had risen from the dead. What does this attitude shift and subsequent resolve on the part of the disciples convey about the authenticity of the resurrection? If the disciples hadn't really seen Jesus alive, what could account for their change of heart and heroic efforts to spread the gospel? How likely do you think that the disciples were sincere, but sincerely wrong?

5. The disciples were in the unique position of knowing for certain whether Jesus had returned from the dead, and they were willing to die for their conviction that he had. Can you think of anyone in history who has knowingly and willingly died for a lie? What degree of certainty would you need before you would be willing to lay down your life for a belief? How thoroughly would you investigate a matter if you were going to base your life on it? Elaborate.

"I say unequivocally that the evidence for the resurrection of Jesus Christ is so overwhelming that it compels acceptance by proof which leaves absolutely no room for doubt."

Sir Lionel Luckhoo, called the world's most successful
lawyer by *The Guinness Book of World Records*

Think About This!

"It had been put to me this way: People will die for their religious beliefs if they sincerely believe they're true, but people won't die for their religious beliefs if they know their beliefs are false. While most people can only have faith that their beliefs are true, the disciples were in a position to know without a doubt whether or not Jesus had risen from the dead. They claimed that they saw him, talked with him, and ate with him. If they weren't absolutely certain, they wouldn't have allowed themselves to be tortured to death for proclaiming that the resurrection had happened."

Lee Strobel

6. Do you agree or disagree with each of the following statements? Give reasons for your responses.

- People are sometimes willing to die for something they believe is true.

- People are not willing to die for something they *know* to be untrue.

- The disciples were in a unique position in history to *know* the truth about the resurrection.

- The disciples would not willingly die for a hoax or conspiracy regarding the resurrection. (Eleven of twelve disciples were martyred for their faith.)

Think About This!

More Circumstantial Evidence

The Conversion of Skeptics

"Another piece of circumstantial evidence is that there were hardened skeptics who didn't believe in Jesus before his crucifixion — and were to some degree dead-set against Christianity — who turned around and adopted the Christian faith after Jesus' death. There's no good reason for this apart from them having experienced the resurrected Christ."

J. P. Moreland, PhD

The Emergence of the Church

"The resurrection was undoubtedly the central proclamation of the early church from the very beginning. The earliest Christians didn't just endorse Jesus' teachings; they were convinced they had seen him alive after his crucifixion. That's what changed their lives and started the church. Certainly, since this was their centermost conviction, they would have made absolutely sure that it was true."

Gary Habermas, PhD

Ongoing Encounters with Christ

"There's one other category of evidence.... It's the ongoing encounter with the resurrected Christ that happens all over the world, in every culture, people from all kinds of backgrounds and personalities — well educated and not, rich and poor, thinkers and feelers, men and women. They all will testify that more than any single thing in their lives, Jesus Christ has changed them. To me, this provides the final evidence — not the only evidence but the final confirming proof — that the message of Jesus can open the door to a direct encounter with the risen Christ."

J. P. Moreland

Optional Discussion Questions

- Did you have the opportunity to read the content in *The Case for Christ* that corresponds to this session? Based on the circumstantial evidence for the resurrection you've examined so far, what conclusions, if any, can you draw about its validity?

- J. P. Moreland suggests that it is very difficult to explain away the radical transformation of people who were originally skeptical about Jesus and then believed in him after the resurrection. Do you agree with this reasoning? Why or why not? What might have led to the radical transformation of such skeptics as James, the brother of Jesus, and Paul, formerly known as Saul?

- If Jesus had *not* risen from the grave, what did the disciples have to gain — money, power, or status — by falsely professing that he had?

- Besides the resurrection, what might account for the rapid spread of Christianity in spite of the shameful death of its founder and the dispersion of the disciples?

- What is the difference between dying for something you wrongly believe is true and dying for something that you know is untrue? Would anyone sane willingly die for something they knew wasn't true? Why or why not? Do you think the disciples would willingly die for the cause of Jesus if they knew his resurrection were a hoax? What's the possibility that the disciples truly believed, but were really deceived?

- What is the difference between the early disciples who were tortured and/or killed for refusing to renounce their beliefs and suicide bombers today who take their own lives in an attempt to kill others based on their beliefs?

- How do the claims of people worldwide who say they've had a personal experience with the risen Christ influence your opinion of the circumstantial evidence of the case for Christ? Have you ever personally observed someone transform in behavior and character after coming to believe in Jesus Christ? What is your view of people who make such claims?

- J. P. Moreland remarks: "First, I'm not saying, 'Just trust your experience.' I'm saying, 'Use your mind calmly and weigh the evidence, and then let experience be a confirming piece of evidence.' Second, if what this evidence points to is true—that is, if all these lines of evidence really do point to the resurrection of Jesus—the evidence itself begs for an experiential test." What would it take before you would be willing to put Jesus to the test and take the step of inviting him into your life?

WATCH THIS!

DVD Teaching Segment #2

Think About This!

Lee's Story, Part 1

"I'll admit it: I was ambushed by the amount and quality of the evidence that Jesus is the unique Son of God. As I sat at my desk that Sunday afternoon, I shook my head in amazement. I had seen defendants carted off to the death chamber on much less convincing proof! The cumulative facts and data pointed unmistakably toward a conclusion that I wasn't entirely comfortable in reaching. Frankly, I had wanted to believe that the deification of Jesus was the result of legendary development in which well-meaning but misguided people slowly turned a wise sage into the mythological Son of God. That seemed safe and reassuring; after all, a roving apocalyptic preacher from the first century could make no demands on me. But while I went into my investigation thinking that this legendary explanation was intuitively obvious, I emerged convinced it was totally without basis.

"On November 8, 1981, I realized that my biggest objection to Jesus also had been quieted by the evidence of history. I found myself chuckling at how the tables had been turned. In light of the convincing facts I had learned during my investigation, in the face of this overwhelming avalanche of evidence in the case for Christ, the great irony was this: it would require much more faith for me to maintain my atheism than to trust in Jesus of Nazareth!"

DISCUSS THIS!

7. How well do you feel you've been able to investigate the identity of Jesus and the claims of Christianity with an open mind? Do you agree with Lee's observation (see "Think About This!" box on page 104) that there is an avalanche of evidence pointing toward the truth of Christianity? Why or why not? Name some of the most convincing pieces of evidence you have discovered. What questions remain for you?

For God so loved the world that he gave his one and only Son, that whoever believes in him shall not perish but have eternal life. For God did not send his Son into the world to condemn the world, but to save the world through him. Whoever believes in him is not condemned, but whoever does not believe stands condemned already because they have not believed in the name of God's one and only Son.

John 3:16–18

Think About This!

Lee's Story, Part 2

"By November 8, 1981, my legend thesis, to which I had doggedly clung for so many years, had been thoroughly dismantled. What's more, my journalistic skep-

ticism toward the supernatural had melted in light of the breathtaking historical evidence that the resurrection of Jesus was a real, historical event. In fact, my mind could not conjure up a single explanation that fit the evidence of history nearly as well as the conclusion that Jesus was who he claimed to be: the one and only Son of God. The atheism I had embraced for so long buckled under the weight of historical truth. It was a stunning and radical outcome, certainly not what I had anticipated when I embarked on this investigative process. But it was, in my opinion, a decision compelled by the facts. All of which led me to the 'So what?' question. If this is true, what difference does it make? There were several obvious implications."

8. Lee identifies the following list of implications to the "So what?" question concerning the true identity of Jesus. How do these statements strike you? What questions do they raise for you? Which of these statements, if true, would make the greatest impact on your life and why?

   • If Jesus is the Son of God, his teachings are more than just good ideas from a wise teacher; they are divine insights on which I can confidently build my life.

   • If Jesus sets the standard for morality, I can now have an unwavering foundation for my choices and decisions, rather than basing them on the ever-shifting sands of expediency and self-centeredness.

   • If Jesus did rise from the dead, he's still alive today and available for me to encounter on a personal basis.

   • If Jesus conquered death, he can open the door of eternal life for me, too.

   • If Jesus has divine power, he has the supernatural ability to guide me and help me and transform me as I follow him.

   • If Jesus personally knows the pain of loss and suffering, he can comfort and encourage me in the midst of the turbulence that he himself warned is inevitable in a world corrupted by sin.

   • If Jesus loves me as he says, he has my best interests at heart. That means I have nothing to lose and everything to gain by committing myself to him and his purposes.

- If Jesus is who he claims to be (and remember, no leader of any other major religion has even pretended to be God), as my Creator he rightfully deserves my allegiance, obedience, and worship.

Think About This!

Lee's Story, Part 3

"After a personal investigation that spanned more than six hundred days and countless hours, my own verdict in the case for Christ was clear. However, as I sat at my desk, I realized that I needed more than an intellectual decision. I wanted to take the experiential step that J. P. Moreland had described in my interview with him. Looking for a way to bring that about, I reached over to a Bible and opened it to John 1:12, a verse I had encountered during my investigation: 'Yet to all who did receive him, to those who believed in his name, he gave the right to become children of God.' The key verbs in that verse spell out with mathematical precision what it takes to go beyond mere mental assent to Jesus' deity and enter into an ongoing relationship with him by becoming adopted into God's family: believe + receive = become."

9. According to John 1:12 (see box above), what does it take to become a child of God? What does it mean to *believe* in Jesus Christ? What do you think it means to *receive* Jesus into your life? What does it mean to *become* a child of God?

Think About This!

Lee's Story, Part 4

"When I read in the Bible that my sins separated me from God, who is holy and morally pure, this resonated as being true. Certainly God, whose existence I had denied for years, seemed extremely distant, and it became obvious to me that I needed the cross of Jesus to bridge that gulf. Said the apostle Peter, 'For Christ died for sins once for all, the righteous for the unrighteous, to bring you to God' (1 Peter 3:18 NIV).

"Every other faith system I studied during my investigation was based on the 'do' plan. In other words, it was necessary for people to do something — for example, use a Tibetan prayer wheel, pay alms, go on pilgrimages, undergo re-incarnations, work off karma from past misdeeds, reform their character — to try to somehow earn their way back to God. Despite their best efforts, lots of sincere people just wouldn't make it. Christianity is unique. It's based on the 'done' plan — Jesus has done for us on the cross what we cannot do for ourselves: he has paid the death penalty that we deserve for our rebellion and wrongdoing, so we can become reconciled with God."

10. To what extent can you relate to Lee's sense of being separated from God because of sin? Lee explains that every other faith system is based on the "do" plan, but Christianity alone is based on what has already been "done." Read his comments again and summarize his points in your own words. What is it that Jesus did on the cross that we cannot do for ourselves?

For the wages of sin is death, but the gift of God is eternal life in Christ Jesus our Lord.

Romans 6:23

Think About This!

Lee's Story, Part 5

"Once the 'believe' part of John 1:12 is firmly in place, all that's left is to 'receive' Jesus' grace, and then you'll become his son or daughter, engaged in a spiritual adventure that can flourish for the rest of your life and into eternity.

"So on November 8, 1981, I talked with God in a heartfelt and unedited prayer, admitting and turning from my wrongdoing, and receiving the gift of forgiveness and eternal life through Jesus. I told him that with his help I wanted to follow him and his ways from here on out. There were no lightning bolts, no audible replies, no tingly sensations. I know that some people feel a rush of emotion at such a moment; as for me, however, there was something else that was equally exhilarating: there was the rush of reason.

"Looking back nearly two decades, I can see with clarity that the day I personally made a decision in the case for Christ was nothing less than the pivotal event of my entire life. After taking that step, I knew from John 1:12 that I had crossed the threshold into a new experience. I had 'become' something different: a child of God, forever adopted into his family through the historical, risen Jesus. Said the apostle Paul, 'Therefore, if anyone is in Christ, he is a new creation; the old has gone, the new has come' (2 Corinthians 5:17 NIV)."

11. What is your verdict in the case for Christ? To what extent has the evidence presented in these sessions (and the book *The Case for Christ*) been sufficient for you to draw a final conclusion? Are you willing to take a step in the direction the evidence is pointing and place your faith and trust in Jesus Christ, receiving him into your life? If not, what obstacles or barriers are most holding you back? What kinds of questions remain for you?

12. In what ways, either positively or negatively, might your life change if you were to follow Jesus? What do you think would be the most difficult part about it? What would be the most thrilling part for you?

WATCH THIS!

DVD Wrap-up/Lee's Perspective

For it is by grace you have been saved, through faith — and this not from yourselves, it is the gift of God — not by works, so that no one can boast.

Ephesians 2:8 – 9

IN THE COMING DAYS

Personal Reflection

Yet to all who did receive him, to those who believed in his name, he gave the right to become children of God.

John 1:12

BELIEVE + RECEIVE = BECOME

- To what extent have you been able to set aside your biases and preconceived notions and approach the evidence in these discussions as a fair and impartial juror in the case for Christ? In the end, the verdict is yours and yours alone. Nobody else can cast the ballot for you.

- After examining the experts, considering the arguments, and discussing your concerns, maybe you have the "believe" part of the above equation down, and all that's left for you is to "receive" the forgiveness, grace, and leadership of Jesus Christ in your life. What does it mean for you to receive Jesus? How might this impact your life? How does the idea of becoming a "son" or "daughter" of God make you feel? Does it seem a little mystical or does it fill you with hope and wonder? Are you willing to take that step in a simple, unrehearsed prayer to God right now?

- Or, on the other hand, do you still have lingering questions, doubts, or concerns? Perhaps the case isn't conclusive and you have unresolved issues that haven't been addressed. If so, are you willing to continue on in your investigative journey by checking out some of the related resources suggested in the book? Or if you've benefited from this format, your next step might be to consider a discussion on *The Case for Faith* or *The Case for a Creator.*

- Whatever your conclusion, are you willing to make this a front-burner issue in your life? If Jesus really is who he claimed to be, your eternal life hinges on it, for as he himself said, "If you do not believe that I am the one I claim to be, you will indeed die in you sins" (John 8:24 NIV). These are sobering words, but they were offered by Jesus out of an authentic and loving concern for each one of us. So we urge you to carefully and seriously consider all of the evidence presented and ultimately answer this final question: *What is your verdict in the case for Christ?*

Jesus [said], "I am the way and the truth and the life. No one comes to the Father except through me."

John 14:6

Therefore, if anyone is in Christ, he is a new creation; the old has gone, the new has come!

2 Corinthians 5:17 NIV

Share Your Thoughts

With the Author: Your comments will be forwarded to the author when you send them to *zauthor@zondervan.com*.

With Zondervan: Submit your review of this book by writing to *zreview@zondervan.com*.

Free Online Resources at
www.zondervan.com/hello

 Zondervan AuthorTracker: Be notified whenever your favorite authors publish new books, go on tour, or post an update about what's happening in their lives.

 Daily Bible Verses and Devotions: Enrich your life with daily Bible verses or devotions that help you start every morning focused on God.

 Free Email Publications: Sign up for newsletters on fiction, Christian living, church ministry, parenting, and more.

 Zondervan Bible Search: Find and compare Bible passages in a variety of translations at www.zondervanbiblesearch.com.

 Other Benefits: Register yourself to receive online benefits like coupons and special offers, or to participate in research.

ZONDERVAN®
.com